English for the Hotel Industry

Aysha Viswamohan

PEARSON

Delhi • Chennai

Editor—ELT: Romila Saha
Assistant Editor—Production: Sonam Arora

ISBN 978-81-317-7356-7

First Impression

Published by Dorling Kindersley (India) Pvt. Ltd, licensees of Pearson Education in South Asia.

Head Office: 7th Floor, Knowledge Boulevard, A-8(A), Sector 62, Noida, UP 201309, India.
Registered Office: 11 Community Centre, Panchsheel Park, New Delhi 110017, India.

Compositor: White Lotus Infotech Pvt. Ltd.
Printed in India by Sterling Graphics. Pvt. Ltd.

To my family

Contents

Foreword

I am delighted to have this opportunity to support this very useful and practical course book, *English for the Hotel Industry*.

Language communication ability can be defined as the ability to apply general language knowledge to specific contexts of use. It is often stated that general English is taught for no particular purpose; therefore it is extremely important that applied linguistic knowledge be successfully used in practical fields which not only support local economies but also promote relations with other countries. Thinking globally but acting locally is the essence of our modern world and through this book, Dr Viswamohan has made an excellent contribution to this practical philosophy of internationally-oriented teaching.

The syllabus of *English for the Hotel Industry* includes interesting case studies, and builds in the three essentials of language learning and teaching: focus on context, focus on language form and focus on language skills or functions. It focuses on the inclusion of a wide range of topics related to the hospitality industry–from ordering a taxi to handling emergencies.

I am convinced that this book will be useful both as an independent course for hospitality professionals and as a practical supplement to standard general English courses which need to add a real-life component. It is informative, well-designed and easy to use. Enjoy using it.

Dr Roger Nunn
Chief Editor, *Asian EFL Journal*
and
Professor, The Petroleum Institute, Abu Dhabi

About the Author

Aysha Viswamohan teaches in the Department of Humanities and Social Sciences at the Indian Institute of Technology Madras. She did her postgraduate diploma in Teaching English and M.Phil (ELT) from the English and Foreign Languages University, Hyderabad. She did her Ph.D. on the works of the American playwright, Arthur Miller. Her teaching and research interests are Drama, Communication and Film Studies. Her books include *English for Technical Communication* (2007) and *English for Nurses* (2010).

Acknowledgements

I would like to thank Professor Bhaskar Ramamurthy, Director, IIT Madras; and Professor Ajit Kolar, Chairman, Centre for Continuing Education, IIT Madras, for providing the facilities and infrastructure for this endeavour.

I am thankful to Professor Roger Nunn for graciously writing the foreword.

I am grateful to the faculty and staff of the Department of Humanities and Social Sciences, IIT Madras. I also acknowledge the library staff of IIT Madras; Simon Fraser University, Vancouver, Canada; British Council, Chennai; and the English and Foreign Languages University, Hyderabad. I also thank my students and research scholars.

My thanks also go to the Pearson publishing team: Ritu Chaudhri, Shreya Roy Chowdhury, Romila Saha and Sonam Arora.

Finally, a special thanks to my family: my son Aneesh, husband Viswamohan, mother Dr (Mrs) M. Iqbal and my father, (late) Dr Iqbal Ahmed.

Aysha Viswamohan
Indian Institute of Technology Madras

Introduction

English for the Hotel Industry is meant for those professionals who work in the hospitality industry, interact with corporate and international clients, aim to go and work in English-speaking countries, or just want to improve their English language abilities. Essentially, it simulates situations where you might need English to talk to your clients, guests, tourists, and customers.

English for the Hotel Industry focuses on the language and communication skills that you need in professional situations. The activities and situations emphasize the essential elements of language: listening, speaking, reading, and writing, with plenty of vocabulary and pronunciation practice. The book attempts to develop the language and interpersonal skills essential for having a successful career in a high profile industry.

The course is divided into 15 chapters and helps you to handle a variety of situations politely, from making a reservation and handling complaints to helping guests explore the town.

The case studies at the end of the comprehensive chapters will enable you to deal with different types of travellers, including businesspeople and holidaymakers, and with situations demanding an increased level of sensitivity.

English for the Hotel Industry makes effective use of hospitality terminology. You will be encouraged to use your professional expertise; however, the primary motive of this book is not to teach hotel management skills. Our intention is to encourage you to use the English language in professional and social situations skillfully. If you are already working or aspire to work in the hotel industry, and English is the language of communication, then *English for the Hotel Industry* will help you in all your professional needs.

The book can be used in the classroom or individually; however, since language is a social skill, it is advisable to use it with a partner.

What Does *English for the Hotel Industry* Contain?

Listening

The CD for developing your listening skills consists of excerpts on a range of topics. After listening, you must attempt the questions that follow. All activities are based on the passages you have listened to from the recording.

Speaking

Speaking activities in this book focus on aspects of customer care and professional situations needed in an English-speaking environment. The speaking activities involve role plays, individual presentations, pair work and group discussions, which provide opportunities to talk and exchange information and views. The role plays are especially designed to help you practise speaking with friends and colleagues, thus enabling you to speak more confidently in all real life situations.

Reading

In this book, you will find reading passages related to hospitality, travel and tourism, and situations which you may generally encounter in your professional life. The reading activities and exercises include activities which are pre-reading, and post-reading. The 'Appreciating Literature' section is our way of using literature for teaching/learning English. This section will not only break the monotony of reading passages strictly based on professional situations, but also help you engage great minds of all ages. All tasks and activities that follow are designed to develop not just reading, but also writing and speaking skills, with lots of vocabulary and grammar exercises.

Writing

Writing is an important function of communication, and this book is aware of the importance of this skill. Activities which are directly related to your profession include writing e-mails, faxes, memos and résumés.

Vocabulary

English for the Hotel Industry will also help you expand and enrich your vocabulary. It engages you in understanding meaning through contexts, while encouraging you to use a dictionary to locate meanings of words you may not be familiar with.

The author wishes you all the best in your efforts towards learning English.

1

Making a Hotel Reservation

Situation
- Reserving a room for a guest
- Know your way around the hotel

Speaking
- Hotel-related expressions and vocabulary

Grammar Bin
- Using *through* and *to*
- Using contractions
- Short answers with *be*
- Subject pronouns and possessive adjectives

Real-life Reads
- Advertisements

Language Focus
- Handling complaints and making suggestions

Reading Comprehension
- Describing a hotel

Writing
- Writing advertisements
- E-mail writing

Pronunciation Practice
- Numbers and /-sh/ sound

Appreciating Literature
- *London* by William Blake

SITUATION

Reserving a Room for a Guest

Amar Ghodke is a businessman in Pune. He has to visit Bangalore for a business meeting. He usually prefers to stay in Hotel Central in Bangalore. He calls them up.

Read and practise the following conversation:

Desk Clerk: Good morning. Reception, Hotel Central. How may I help you?
Amar: Good morning. I'm Amar Ghodke, calling from Pune. I wonder if I could reserve* a room, single, with breakfast and meals included, for a week, from 24 August *onwards*?
Desk Clerk: Certainly sir, could you please give me your phone number?
Amar: It's 9876654321.
Desk Clerk: Thank you, sir. May I request you to hold the phone for a moment while I check for availability? ... I'm extremely sorry, Mr Ghodke, but we're in the middle of an international medical conference during the period you've mentioned, and are rather short of rooms. We'd therefore be unable to provide a single room.
Amar: Well, in that case, could you suggest any *alternative*, please?
Desk Clerk: Would you like to go for our regular plan? Here you pay for your accommodation, breakfast and one meal. However, you won't be getting full meals.
Amar: Hmm, I wouldn't mind that. I guess I'll go for it.
Desk Clerk: Very well, Mr Ghodke (*types in the details*). You have a confirmed reservation with us from the 24th of August through the 30th. May I know what time you would *check in*?
Amar: Around 9.30 in the morning, I believe, if the flight's at the right time. And there is one more thing. I'd like to have a room with a balcony.
Desk Clerk: That can be easily arranged for. And can I have your address and your contact number, please?
Amar: Of course. It's 36, AR Apartments, Kalyani Nagar, Pune.
Desk Clerk: Thank you sir, we look forward to your visit. Have a safe journey.
Amar: Thank you.

* In American English, the word *reserve* is used booking a hotel room, whereas British English mostly uses *book* a room.

Essential Vocabulary

Table 1.1 Meanings of Common Expressions

SL. NO.	EXPRESSION	MEANING
1	Call somebody up	To speak to someone over the phone
2	24th onwards	Starting from the 24th
3	Alternative	The choice between two possibilities
4	Check in	Arriving at a hotel or guest house

Know Your Way Around a Hotel

Exercise 1

Choose the words given in the box below and fill in the blanks. Consult a dictionary for answers:

Cashier	Chef	Banqueting manager
Bartender	Bell desk	Receptionist
Concierge		

i. A person who makes sure that everything in the guests' room is in proper order: _________
ii. A person who discusses arrangements for parties and receptions: _________
iii. A person who prepares the guests' bills: _________
iv. A person who takes care of the wine, liquor and spirits: _________
v. A person who plans the cooking and manages the kitchen: _________
vi. A person who replies to requests made for the reservation of rooms: _________
vii. A person who helps the guests by dealing with luggage and making travel arrangements: _________

Exercise 2

Fill in the blanks with words from the earlier list:

i. Good evening, this is_________ May I help you?
Yes. I'm checking out this evening, please ask the _________ to prepare my bills. And yes, please direct the _________ to confirm my travel plans.
ii. Good afternoon, may I please speak to your _________ _________ You see, I would like to discuss the programme for today's party.
iii. (*Knock, knock*) Who is it?
Good morning, madam. This is Sarah, the _________ _________, with your morning tea.
iv. The food was excellent.
Thank you, sir. I shall convey your compliments to the _________.

SPEAKING

Hotel-Related Expressions and Vocabulary

Perform the following role play. Assume the role of a desk clerk, with your friend playing the guest. Prepare a conversation using the following words:

Non-smoking	Bellboy	Room service
Swimming pool	Pets	Crib
Credit card	Rollaway (bed)	Baby-sitter
Vending machine	Tariff	Restaurant

GRAMMAR BIN

Using *through* and *to*

Usage: In the conversation above, we have seen the use of the expression '24th August *through* the 30th'. This is an American usage denoting a period of time, inclusive of both dates given. The usage has the advantage of meaning unambiguously 'up to and including' the dates mentioned. The British usage, for example, '24th August to 30th', can sometimes be confusing as to whether the final date is to be included or not.

Short Answers with *be*

Table 1.2 Short Questions and Answers

QUESTION	ANSWER
What's your name?	My name is Josephine
Where are you working?	I'm working at AR Suites
Who's that?	His name is Satwik
What's her name?	Her name is Aditi
Where's she from?	She's from Shimla
What are their names?	Their names are Harsh, Gaurav, Devkanya and Gautami
Note: The various forms of the verb *be* and their uses: am: I am a manager. is: She is a receptionist. are: They are chefs.	

USING CONTRACTIONS	SUBJECT PRONOUNS	POSSESSIVE ADJECTIVES
I am = I'm	I	My
You are = You're	You	Your
He is = He's	He	His
She is = He's	She	Her
It is = It's	It	Its
What is = What's	They	Their

REAL-LIFE READS

Advertisements

Pre-reading Activity
Read a few advertisements about service apartments in your city. Discuss the facilities provided by them.

Reading

Read the advertisements for the following service apartments and answer the questions below:

Advertisements

a. Star Apartments

We have 12 suites, 1bhk/ 2bhk fully furnished, equipped kitchen, toilet, terrace 20 m sq. ft, 7th floor, elevator, parking lot, plenty of greenery around the apartments. Write to: M.K. Raghav, 54, Sanghi St, Ranchi. Mobile: 95750-45606. E-mail: starapts@gmail.com

b. Grand Apartment

We have seven suites, 1bhk, all ground floor, parking lot, plenty of walking area. Write to: W. Glover, 1221 Richie Street, Puducherry. Cell: 98566-73454.

c. The Royal Gardens

We have six rooms, fully furnished, attached toilet, swimming pool, parking facility, fully-equipped gymnasium, peaceful locality. Write to: Nitin Bhatt, 99 West Street, Jayanagar, Bangaluru. Cell: 87765-04477. Email: bhatt@airtel.in

d. Orchid

We have six semi-detached houses, three rooms/kitchen/toilet, *prkg. avail.*, common swimming pool, main street, two blocks from the central railway station. Write to: Gisela Cruz, Orchid, 96 Marine Road, Chennai. Phone: 044-5759-5005.

Exercise 1

Answer the following questions:

i. Sylvia has a heart problem and the doctor has asked her to avoid any kind of exertion. As her travel agent, which apartment would you recommend to her?
ii. Cruz is very athletic. What kind of accommodation would he go for?
iii. Charu is travelling alone and loves greenery. Which apartment would she prefer?
iv. Emily is a writer and needs to work quietly. Which house would you suggest for her?
v. What do you understand by 'prkg.avail.'?

Dictionary Work

Find out the meanings of the following words using a dictionary:

Equipped kitchen	BHK
Suites	Main street

LANGUAGE FOCUS

Handling Complaints and Making Suggestions

Read the following expressions aloud and discuss their significance:

Table 1.3 More Common Expressions

EXPRESSIONS	SIGNIFICANCE
May I request you to hold on?	Request which suggests that the caller should wait for a while as the person at the other end of the line is busy.
Please	Request for something
I'm extremely sorry.	Apologizing
I wonder if I could…	Starting to make a request
Goodbye	Taking leave of someone
Have a safe journey.	Wishing somebody who is going on a journey

In the dialogue in the Situation segment, we have seen the way the desk clerk answers the client's queries with courtesy and patience. It is important for an employee to present his/her company in the best light. For this, he should be able to handle complaints effectively, along with taking responsibility for a mistake and apologizing for the inconvenience caused to patrons.

Example: *Your complaint is justified* and I shall look into the matter immediately. I'm extremely sorry, but the hotel is full. *Would you like us to* suggest an alternative?

Exercise 1
Look at the following sentences and fill in the blanks with the appropriate ones given in the box:

i. I'm afraid, I do not handle this department ___________
ii. About the missing baggage, ___________
iii. Hotel Mascot ___________
iv. We are so sorry about the confusion regarding your reservation ___________
v. It appears that there is an error in your bill ___________

a. There seems to have been a mistake at our end.
b. We shall do our best to locate it.
c. May we request you to give us a few minutes while we correct it?
d. May I help you?
e. Perhaps you'd like to speak to Mr Noah about it.

Exercise 2
Match the conversations in the following columns:

SL. NO.	CLIENT	SL. NO.	STAFF
i.	Where can I get some fresh cookies?	a.	I'm extremely sorry, sir/madam. We will send a plumber to fix the *faucet* immediately
ii.	Please pull down the *blinds**, it's rather sunny	b.	I'm sending the bellboy to get your bags down
iii.	The tap is leaking badly	c.	Certainly, sir/madam
iv.	The hairdryer is not working	d.	Our bakery has the best cookies in town. We can get you some right away
v.	I need help with my luggage	e.	I'm extremely sorry, sir/madam. We'll replace it immediately
**faucet* = tap **blinds* = curtains			

READING COMPREHENSION

Describing a Hotel

Pre-reading Activity
Discuss how important the location of a hotel is for its business.

Reading

Read the following and answer the questions given below:

Advertisements

Villa Woodland

Completely renovated, Villa Woodland is the ideal location to enjoy your stay in Gurgaon, whether on a business trip or for leisure. The contemporarily decorated rooms, warm and well-equipped, the courtesy and professionalism of the staff characterize our hotel. In an ideal area for both ease of access and a friendly atmosphere, a vibrant and secure location, Villa Woodland Hotel is the address that one seeks for an enjoyable stay. As it is in a quiet area, you will enjoy the atmosphere of a village, while in a hotel. Borrowing from nature, this hotel, with modern rooms in attractive colours, guarantees you rest, comfort and attentive service.

Rooms

The Villa has 32 rooms, including four executive rooms, all fully renovated in 2012 to combine comfort, luxury and modernity. Divided into three categories, all rooms are equipped with quality bedding and duvets (double or twin rooms). The bathrooms and showers enjoy natural daylight.

Classic Rooms

True gems furnished with double beds and duvets, the classic rooms provide every comfort for both business and leisure stays.

Superior Rooms
Ideal for a getaway for two, the superior rooms offer more space and therefore, are ideal for more ease and comfort. Equipped with double beds or two single beds.

Executive Rooms
A latest 'must have' at the Villa, the executive rooms offers high-end luxury. Quality bedding and duvets, LCD TVs, seating area furnished with sofas, separate toilets and contemporary bathrooms.

In Rooms

- Individually controlled air-conditioning
- Double glazing
- Hair dryer
- Satellite television high definition: more than 80 Hindi and international channels
- Extra cots on request

For Breakfast

The most important meal of the day, the breakfast, an open buffet, is prepared with great care. All the items are carefully selected to offer a healthy meal.

Other Services

- Complimentary Internet wi-fi
- Fax and photocopier at reception
- Dry cleaning and laundry on request, back in a day
- Luggage storage
- Concierge service 24 hours
- 24 hour-car parking at 50 metres' distance with preferential rates
- Cash, Visa, American Express and MasterCard accepted

Exercise 1
Answer the following in one or two sentences:

i. What is special about the hotel's location?

____

____

____

ii. What are the major services provided to the guests?

____

____

____

iii. What are the 'must haves' of the executive rooms?

____

____

____

Exercise 2

State whether the following are true or false:

i. The rooms in the hotel are divided into three categories. ____________

ii. The hotel does not have a buffet breakfast. ____________

iii. Internet service is available only with additional fee. ____________

WRITING

Writing an Advertisement

As the media manager of a star hotel, you have to prepare an advertisement highlighting the features of your hotel. You may include the following:

Ambience	Services
Location	Rooms
Shopping centre	Restaurant

Create your advertisement in the following space:

Writing an E-mail

You received the following e-mail from the Secretary to the Chairman, Universal Electronics, requesting you to make some changes in the room reserved from 12 February through 16 February, in the name of R. K. Vyas, Chairman, Universal Electronics.

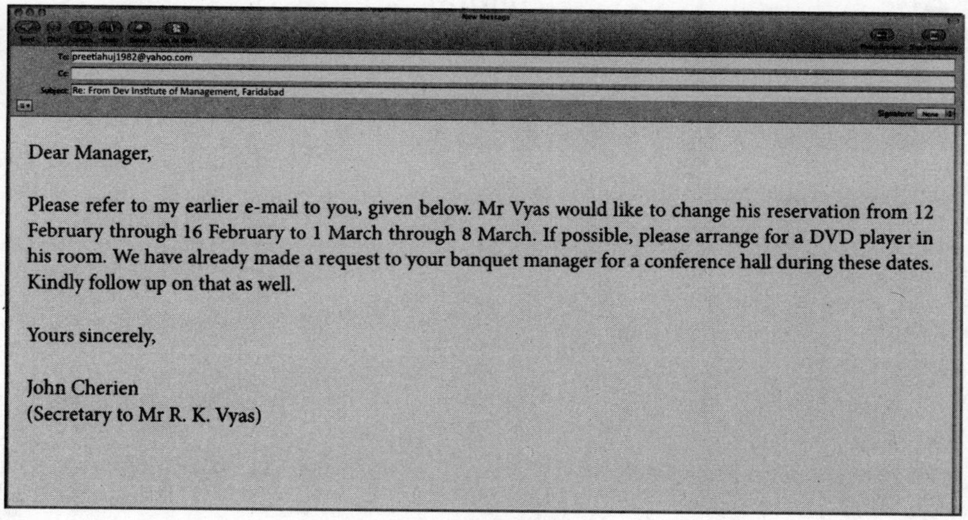

To: preetiahuj1982@yahoo.com

Cc:

Subject: Re: From Dev Institute of Management, Faridabad

Dear Manager,

Please refer to my earlier e-mail to you, given below. Mr Vyas would like to change his reservation from 12 February through 16 February to 1 March through 8 March. If possible, please arrange for a DVD player in his room. We have already made a request to your banquet manager for a conference hall during these dates. Kindly follow up on that as well.

Yours sincerely,

John Cherien
(Secretary to Mr R. K. Vyas)

Now write a response to the e-mail. Your e-mail should highlight:

- Availability of the room during these dates
- Arranging of a DVD player
- Following up on the conference hall

PRONUNCIATION PRACTICE

Numbers and the /-sh/ Sound

Practise the pronunciation of the following words:

Table 1.4 Pronunciation

NUMBERS	/-sh/ SOUND
Twenty- fourth	Demi-pension
Thirteenth	Reservation
Twelve hundred	International
Three hundred and nine	Accommodation
Fifty-five thousand	Mentioned
Two thousand and thirty three	Mansion
Sixty thousand and four hundred	Confirmation

APPRECIATING LITERATURE

Read the following poem by William Blake:

London

By *William Blake*

I wander thro' each charter'd street,
Near where the charter'd Thames does flow,
And mark in every face I meet
Marks of weakness, marks of woe.

In every cry of every Man,
In every Infant's cry of fear,
In every voice, in every ban,
The mind-forg'd manacles I hear.

How the Chimney-sweeper's cry
Every black'ning Church appalls;
And the hapless Soldier's sigh
Runs in blood down Palace walls.

But most thro' midnight streets I hear
How the youthful Harlot's curse
Blasts the new born Infant's tear,
And blights with plagues the Marriage hearse.

William Blake (1757–1827), English artist, mystic and poet wrote Songs of Innocence *(1789) and* Songs of Experience *(1794).*

Culture

Exercise 1

The following are the meanings of a few difficult words taken from the poem. Look up their complete meanings in a dictionary and make notes below each word. Can you find any synonyms for them? Why is the word 'chartered' contracted here? Discuss with your teacher and your peers.

- Charter'd: marked, mapped

  ____

  ____

- Appalls: repulses

  ____

  ____

- Manacles: a device for confining hands

  ____

  ____

- Harlot: a woman of bad reputation

- Hearse: a carriage used to carry coffins

Making Presentations

You make presentations everyday—to your teacher, your boss, even your peers and family. You will probably need to make presentations in your professional life too, wherein you will try to introduce, inform and convince your audience about some idea or the other.

Here are a few questions which you can ask yourself before making a presentation:

- Which media will I use for making my presentation? Will I only speak or will I be able to use a flip chart or a PowerPoint presentation too? Will I be provided with picture aids?
- How well does my audience understand the topic? What is the level of their language proficiency?
- What is the core idea of my presentation? How do I adhere to it?
- How can I make my audience more comfortable? Can I use humour or introduce topics of discussion from time to time?

Exercise 1

In groups of three or more, make a presentation about your city. Highlight its three strengths and three weaknesses.

You may include the following aspects:

- Popular locations for sightseeing
- Famous food
- Negative aspects of your city, such as pollution and overcrowding
- Ways of improving your city

You can make rough notes for your presentation here:

2

Welcoming a Guest at the Front Desk

Situation

- Greeting a guest at the reception
- Responding to queries about the room

Reading Comprehension

- Hospitality and culture

Grammar Bin

- Numbers: *there is* and *there are*
- Contracted forms: *there's, there isn't* and *there aren't*

Language Focus

- Polite expressions

Vocabulary

- Prefixes

Pronunciation Practice

- Names of countries and cities

Appreciating Literature

- *Westminster Bridge* by William Wordsworth

SITUATION

Greeting a Guest at the Reception

Meera Raman arrives at Hotel Cascade. She confirms her reservation with the receptionist. Read and practise the following conversation:

Receptionist: Good evening, madam.
Meera: Good evening. I have a reservation, in the name of Meera Raman.
Receptionist: Yes, madam. That's a single room for three days?
Meera: That's right.
Receptionist: Could you just sign here, please?
Meera: Sure.
Receptionist: Thank you, madam. Here's your key. It's on the fourth floor, room 407. I'll call the porter, he will guide you to your room. We shall have the baggage sent up to your room in a moment.
Meera: Thank you.
Receptionist: You're welcome. Enjoy your stay.

Responding to Queries About a Room

A guest in a hotel does not like his room and wants it changed. Read and practise the following conversation:

Receptionist: Good morning, sir.
Guest: Hi. Would it be possible to change my room? There's some construction noise in the street behind my room and I had trouble sleeping last night.
Receptionist: We are very sorry for the inconvenience. May we offer you a very quiet room on the top floor?
Guest: That's great. What is it like?
Receptionist: It has a view of the sea. It's very quiet and includes everything you need.
Guest: What about the air-conditioning?
Receptionist: There's full air-conditioning, of course. Would you like to take a look before you shift?
Guest: That would be nice. Can we do it right away?
Receptionist: Sure, sir. I'll ask the bell boy to show you to the room.

Exercise 1
Fill in the blanks with the appropriate words given in the box below:

i. There's a ______________ by the bed.
ii. The ______________ are changed every day.
iii. Please get me a new pair of batteries for the ______________.

iv. There are plenty of coat hangers in the ____________.
v. I'm afraid, there's no ____________ in the room.
vi. There's a ____________ by the window with a reading lamp on it.
vii. There are two ____________ in the room.
viii. The ____________ is set at 6.30 am.
ix. There are chocolates in the ____________.

Beds	Telephone	Desk
Mini bar	Bed sheets	Radio alarm
Remote control	DVD player	Wardrobe

READING COMPREHENSION

Hospitality and Culture

Discussion

How important is cultural awareness in the hospitality industry? What problems can arise if there is a cultural misunderstanding? Discuss in a group.

Pre-reading Activity

Make a list of five things that are taboo in the cultural context of our country/your local area.

Reading

Now read the following passage on inter-cultural greetings:

Handshake or Hug? Knowing Intercultural Greetings

a. Culture is not ethnic or racial. It is learned and we have to appreciate that each culture is different. It is important, therefore, to treat everyone like a unique individual, as you would like to be treated, and not to get fixated on stereotypes. Also, one must develop one's emotional intelligence to be more intuitive about how to communicate with, negotiate with, and interact with people from cultural backgrounds other than one's own.

b. For example, in South Texas, if one is talking to a male, they will stand at a 90 degree angle to the speaker. If you move, your interlocutor will shift too. This is a markedly non-intimate position, and often the eyes are cast down at the floor or out across the floor, not at the other party. South Texans generally say 'Pleased to know you,' while Mid Westerners say, 'Pleased to meet you.' And in San Antonio, Texas—in a strictly social setting—it is not customary to shake hands with women.

c. In a sophisticated society, there's the hug: two women will mime a hug with no part of their body touching, just tapping each other on the back.

d. In business contexts, one should be aware that most of the world does not greet by shaking hands. People from Asian cultures bow in greeting, but the bows are different. People from Cambodia and Laos will often bow with both hands together in front of the chest as if praying.

In Japan, the depth of the bow signifies the level of respect for the other party. Many Koreans prefer bowing and if they shake hands, the right hand is supported at the wrist by the left hand to show respect. Thais bow with palms together about chest-high with their fingers outstretched. And, there are exceptions. The Taiwanese usually nod the head in recognition rather than bow.

e. Some cultures, such as Native Hawaiians and Mexicans, greet by hugging. Immigrant men from the Middle East often shake hands with a slight nod or bow and then exchange kisses on both cheeks. One should shake hands with a Middle Eastern woman only when she extends her hand.

f. In the Middle East, one of the most insulting things you can do is sit with your legs crossed so the bottom of your foot is pointed in the other person's direction. To show someone the bottom of your foot means you are looking for a fight.

g. Even handshaking cultures such as England, France, Germany, Italy and the United States do it differently. If the British prefer a brief but firm handshake, the French prefer a light grip while sharing one gentle single shake that is quickly withdrawn. Germans will give a very firm handshake—just one 'pump' then quick withdrawal. More than one shake with Germans or French is considered aggressive. Italians will shake hands and then hug friends or kiss them on both cheeks.

Still, when in doubt, err on the side of conservatism.

(Adapted from an article on *http://www.bpic.co.uk*)

Exercise 1

Answer the following questions.

i. Suggest an alternative title for the above passage.
ii. In paragraph b, what do you understand by the term 'non-intimate position'?
iii. A society hug is ____________________.
iv. What is the most insulting thing one can do in the Middle East?
v. How do people generally shake hands in Britain?
vi. Explain the line, 'when in doubt, err on the side of conservatism'.

Exercise 2

Match the following:

Table 2.1

SL. NO.	COUNTRY	SL. NO.	STYLE OF BOWLING
i.	Japan	a.	Both hands together in front of the chest as if praying.
ii.	Cambodia	b.	The depth of the bow signifies the level of respect for the other party.
iii.	Korea	c.	Palms together about chest-high with their fingers outstretched.
iv.	Thailand	d.	The right hand is supported at the wrist by the left hand to show respect.

GRAMMAR BIN

Numbers: *There is* and *There are*

We use *there* to introduce topics. The noun following *there* + *be* often has an indefinite meaning. If the noun after *be* is singular, the verb is singular; if the noun is plural, the verb is plural. For example, 'Jerry *is* a well-known writer.' and 'Sheena and Shaan *are* travelling abroad.' In the present context we can think of examples such as, 'There *is* a concert in town today.' and 'There *are* four major artists performing on the stage.'

Contracted Forms: *There's* and *There Aren't*

Consider the following sentences and note the usage of *there's, there isn't* and *there aren't*:

i. *There aren't* many who like pork sorpotel.
ii. *There isn't* any cheese in the fridge.
iii. *There's* a newly renovated business centre on the second floor.
iv. *There's* a car for repair.
v. *There aren't* any chilling units here.
vi. *There isn't* any multifunction scale in working condition.

Exercise 1
Join the following to make meaningful sentences:

There's	flowers in my room.
There aren't	a CD player in the room.
There's	a television in the room.
They isn't	a word in this report which is untrue.

Exercise 2
Rewrite the following sentences using *there's* or *there are* in the beginning:

i. Two chefs are in the kitchen. ______________________________
ii. The bottles of vintage wine are in the cellar. ______________________________
iii. Hot water is in the bathroom. ______________________________
iv. A laptop is on the table. ______________________________
v. A man was at the barbecue. ______________________________

LANGUAGE FOCUS

Polite Expressions

In any business or corporation, the importance of politeness cannot be emphasized enough. This is particularly true of the hospitality industry.

Here are some websites you could consult to learn more:

- www.eslgold.com/speaking/greetings.html
- www.english-at-home.com/speaking/english-greetings/
- www.businessenglishebook.com/Business-English-Greetings-Lesson.htm

Read the following expressions and discuss their significance:

Table 2.2 Various Kinds of Expressions

EXPRESSIONS	SIGNIFICANCE
Good morning	To greet somebody between the early hours of morning and 12 pm.
Good evening	To wish someone after 3 pm.
Good night	To wish.
Thank you	To express thanks over a kind act, on receiving a gift, an information or a compliment (e.g., 'You look good' or 'You maintain your house very well.').
Sorry	Apologizing for a rude action or word, whether intended or not. It is also used to express regret over something.
Excuse me	To interrupt someone who is speaking, to request someone to make way for you. Also, to suggest that you are sorry to disturb somebody.

Exercise 1
Fill in the blanks with the right expressions:

i. ____________________ for calling. How can I help you?
ii. ____________________, aren't you a student of Satyam College of Catering?
iii. ____________________, without this information I would not have been able to reach a decision.
iv. ____________________ for calling you at this late hour, but this is rather important.
v. ____________________ viewers. These are the news headlines at 10 pm.

Dictionary Work
We know that a credit card is a small plastic card that we can use to buy goods and services and pay later. Now, using your dictionary, define the following:

A debit card: ____________________

Traveller's check: ____________________

ATM: ____________________

A lease: ____________________

Transaction: ____________________

VOCABULARY

Prefixes

A prefix is a letter or a group of letters that is added to the beginning of a word to change its meaning. Thus, a word such as *undercooked* changes the meaning of the word *cooked*, and the same can be said of its opposite *overcooked.* 'She is stupid as well as incompetent' is an example of using the negative prefix '-in'. Some other examples of negative prefixes are

- **un**: uncomfortable, unreliable, uncovered
- **dis**: disarm, disloyal, disqualify (but not *disturb, distance, disgust*; all these words are complete by themselves, and do not carry prefixes)
- **il**: illegal, illegible, illiterate and so on

Exercise 1

Given below are some negative prefixes. Form at least five words with each of them:

i. Anti-

____

____

____

____

____

ii. A-

____

____

____

____

____

iii. Im-

____

____

____

____

____

iv. Non-

____

____

____

____

____

v. In-

____

____

____

____

____

Besides negative prefixes, there are several other types as well. Here is a list of prefixes that can help you improve your vocabulary:

Table 2.3 Prefixes

PREFIX	MEANING	EXAMPLES
Auto-	By oneself	Autocracy, autobiography, autotypic, autopilot.
Arch-	Highest, worst	Archangel, archduke, archenemy, archbishop.*
Circum	Around	Circumnavigate, circumlocution, circumfusion, circumscribe
Co-	With	Co-author, correlated, cooperation
Counter-	To reverse action	Deforestation, deindustrialization, demoralize, defrost
Ex-	Former	Ex-president, ex-boyfriend, ex-wife, ex-employer
Fore	Before	Foretell, foresee, foreknowledge, foreskin

PREFIX	MEANING	EXAMPLES
Hyper-	Extremely	Hyper-sensitive, hyper-emotional, hyper-tension, hyper-critical
Be-	With	Be-dazzled, be-wigged, be-spectacled, be-witch
Neo-	New, revived	Neo-Nazi, neo-patriot, neo-Gothic, Neo-Romantics
Micro-	Small	Micro-mini, micro-computer, microscope, micro-wave
Multi-	Many	Multi-national, multi-language, multi-colour, multi-cultural

Exercise 2

Fill in the blanks choosing the words given in the box:

i. If you don't polish the ________________, it'll get tarnished.
ii, If you want to ________________ your linen, use a bleaching agent.
iii. You've spilled tea on the bedcover, now it'll leave a ________________.
iv. Use a ________________ to clean the floor with water.
v. If the carpets are dusty, use a ________________.
vi. If you don't ________________ it, this iron grill will become rusty soon.
vii. During winter, we need a ________________ in the room.
viii. Don't put this shirt in the washing machine, it is for ________________ only.
ix. Don't connect too many appliances to one supply; the ________________ may cause a fire.

A radiator	Vacuum cleaner	Silver
Overloading	Stain	Wet mop
An extractor	Dry cleaning	Grease
Whiten		

PRONUNCIATION PRACTICE

Names of Countries and Cities

Pronounce the names of the following cities/countries:

- Houston
- Los Angeles
- Brunei
- Cannes
- Buenos Aires
- Venezuela
- Istanbul
- Prague
- Kuala Lampur
- Vancouver

APPRECIATING LITERATURE

Read the poem *Westminster Bridge* by William Wordsworth.

Westminster Bridge

By *William Wordsworth*

3 September 1802

Earth has not anything to show more fair:
Dull would he be of soul who could pass by
A sight so touching in its majesty:
This City now doth like a garment wear

The beauty of the morning: silent, bare,
Ships, towers, domes, theatres and temples lie
Open unto the fields, and to the sky,
All bright and glittering in the smokeless air.

Never did sun more beautifully steep
In his first splendour valley, rock, or hill;
Ne'er saw I, never felt, a calm so deep!

The river glideth at his own sweet will:
Dear God! the very houses seem asleep;
And all that mighty heart is lying still!

Culture

William Wordsworth (1770–1850) is a British poet, credited with ushering in the English Romantic movement with the publication of Lyrical Ballads *(1798) in collaboration with Samuel Taylor Coleridge. Among his best-known poems are* Daffodils, Lucy Gray, *and* The Solitary Reaper.

Discussion

Discuss the poem with your class. Compare Wordsworth's attitude towards London in this poem with Blake's views on the city, which you studied in Chapter 1. You can make notes in the space provided.

____

____

____

____

____

____

____

____

3

Checking In

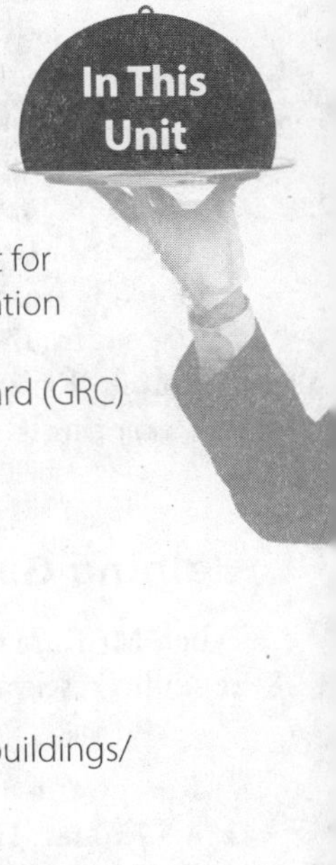

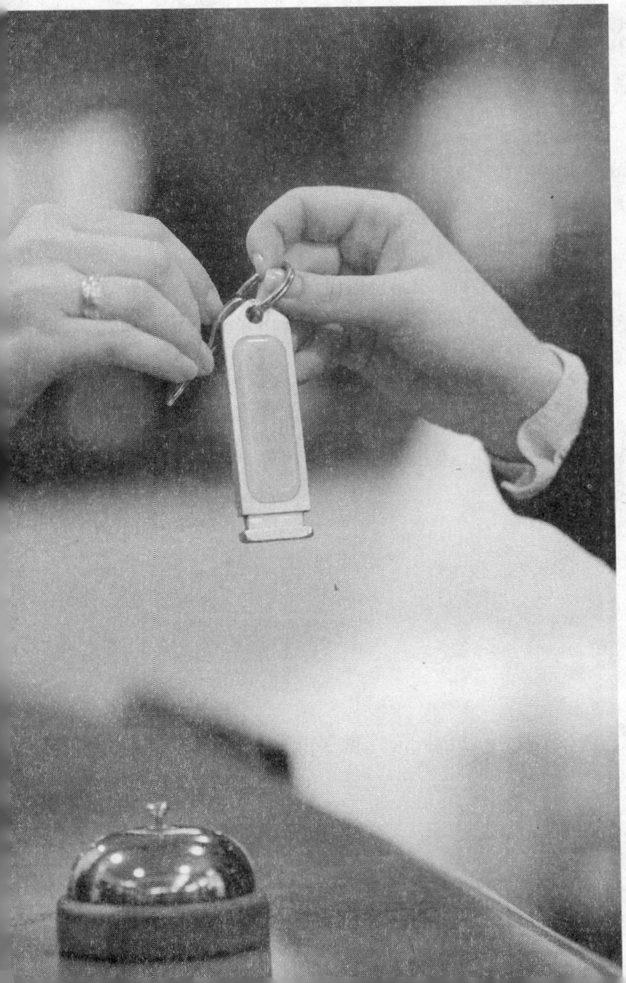

Situation
- Responding to a request for amendment of a reservation
- Helping guests check in
- The guest reservation card (GRC)

Speaking
- Your dream profession

Language Focus
- Politeness markers

Grammar Bin
- About adverbs
- Adjectives: Describing buildings/ structures

Reading Comprehension
- The booming hotel industry

Real-life Reads
- Hotel pamphlets

Writing
- Curriculum vitae
- What is a cover letter?
- Responding to a job Advertisement

Pronunciation Practice
- Percentages

SITUATION

Responding to a Request for Amendment of a Reservation

Narendra Kumar calls up Hotel Regent to change his room preferences and booking date. Read and practise the following conversation:

Receptionist: Good morning. Hotel Regent. How may I help you?
Guest: Hello. I am Narendra Kumar from Jalandhar. I'm calling to change my reservation.
Receptionist: Certainly, Mr Kumar. May we have your phone number please?
Guest: 623626262
Receptionist: Thank you. Let me check your reservation ... Yes sir, you are booked with us. We do have the reservation for a single room for Mrs Kumar and you from the 17th to the 21st. Please tell me your new preference.
Guest: I would like to change my booking from the 19th to the 23rd, and I would like a double room.
Receptionist: Would you please stay on the line while I check for availability? ... Yes sir, we do have a double room through those dates. Shall I book it in your name?
Guest: Sure, thank you.
Receptionist: You are most welcome, Mr Kumar. We are sending you an e-mail confirming the booking from the 19th to the 23rd of April 2012 to nkumar@email.com. Kindly reply to the e-mail to confirm the same.
Guest: Right, I will.
Receptionist: Thank you very much, Mr Kumar. We look forward to having you with us.

Helping Guests Check In

When Mr Kumar and his wife arrive at Hotel Regent, the receptionist gives them general information about his reservation. Read and practise the following conversation:

Receptionist: Good afternoon, sir. Good afternoon, madam.
Mr Kumar: Hello, I'm Narendra Kumar from Jalandhar. I'm booked from the 19th to the 23rd for a double-room. We have a reservation with you.
Receptionist: Yes Mr Kumar, we were expecting you. Your room is confirmed. You'll be in room 309, which is on the third floor.
Mr Kumar: Can I have the keys?
Receptionist: Sure sir, here you are.
Mr Kumar: One more thing. What's the check-out time?
Receptionist: It's 12 noon, sir.
Mr Kumar: Do you have a late check-out?
Receptionist: You can check out till 2 pm. We don't have late check-outs as a norm, but we will be happy to accommodate you.
Mr Kumar: Alright. Which way is the elevator?
Receptionist: Right ahead, sir. The porter is here, he'll carry your luggage and show you the room.
Mr Kumar: Thank you.
Receptionist: You're welcome, sir. Have a pleasant stay with us.

The Guest Reservation Card (GRC)

The following is a standard guest reservation card or form. Go through it carefully, and fill it in exactly as you would expect Narendra Kumar to fill it.

Hotel Regent

15, Lodhi Road, New Delhi-01

Tel: 65765361, 65765360

Personal Particulars

Name (Prof/Dr/Mr/Mrs/Ms) ____________________

Home Address: ____________________

Phone: ____________________ E-mail: ____________________

Designation: ____________________ Organization: ____________________

Office Address: ____________________

Phone: ____________________ Fax: ____________________ E-mail: ____________________

Nationality: ____________________

Passport Number (for foreign nationals only): ____________________

Accommodation Details

Check-in Time: ____________________ Check-out Time: ____________________

Travelling from: ____________________ Travelling to: ____________________

Arrival Date: ____________________ Departure Date: ____________________

Number of Rooms: ____________________ Number of Adults: ________ Children: ____________________

Payment Details

Method of Payment (please select): Cash/ Debit Card/ Credit Card/Cheque

Card (please select): VISA/ MASTERCARD/ AMEX

Card Number: ____________________ Expiry Date: ____________________

Guest Signature ____________ Hotel Manager ____________

SPEAKING

Your Dream Profession

Discuss with your partner the kind of work you do or would like to do in a hotel. Speak in front of the class about it. Discuss the pros and cons of different professions in the hotel industry. You can make notes in the space given below.

Your Work	Your Partner's Work
______	______
______	______
______	______
______	______
______	______
______	______
______	______

LANGUAGE FOCUS

Politeness Markers

We use politeness markers to make requests, express diagreement and to correct people. Choose the appropriate politeness marker from the following box and fill in the blanks:

If I may say so	It's my pleasure to inform you	I'm sorry	Be my guest
I'm afraid	Would you mind	Would you like me to	Certainly, sir

i. Ladies and gentlemen, ________________ that we have the eminent author, Mr Alberto Marquez, among us.

ii. ________________ this is not the correct answer.

iii. ________________ take your coat?

iv. I'm sorry, ________________, but we can surely make amends.

v. The air- conditioner is not working here ________________ moving into another room?

vi. There can be another plan ________________, which is definitely more cost-effective.

vii. 'May I use your phone?'
'________________.'

viii. ________________ for the inconvenience caused.

GRAMMAR BIN

About Adverbs

An *adverb* is a part of speech which modifies adjectives, verbs and clauses. Some common examples of adverbs are:

- originally
- recently
- generally
- frequently
- sufficiently
- continuously
- internationally

All the above words can be classified as *adverbs of manner*. Adverbs of manner tell us *how* something happens. They are usually placed *after the main verb* or *after the object*. We will learn more about adverbs in the next few chapters.

Negative Adverbs

Negative adverbs create a negative meaning in a sentence *without* the use of the usual no/ not/ neither/ nor/never constructions:

- She *seldom* visits her in-laws.
- He *hardly* sleeps since the accident.
- You will *rarely* find her smiling.

Exercise 1

Fill in the blanks with appropriate forms of adverbs:

i. He __________________ goes out. (rare)
ii. The tap has been leaking __________________ (continuous)
iii. The hotel was __________________ owned by the CVR group (origin).
iv. I've been __________________ visiting this hotel (frequent).
v. She's __________________ been to that hotel and was very impressed with the staff (recent).

Adjectives: Describing Buildings/Structures

Consider the following sentence: 'Its distinctive bowed facade, long, horizontal lines and nautical flourishes were striking.' Note the manner in which the building and its parts are described using a variety of adjectives like 'distinctive bowed', 'long, horizontal', etc.

Exercise 1

Now match the adjectives with the most appropriate nouns in the table given below:

SL. NO.	ADJECTIVE	SL. NO.	NOUN
a.	Exclusive	i.	Facilities
b.	Family-friendly	ii.	Retreat
c.	Idyllic tropical	iii.	Rooms
d.	Inter-connecting and non-smoking	iv.	Holidays

READING COMPREHENSION

The Booming Hotel Industry

Pre-reading Activity

In pairs, discuss some important travel destinations in the world. If you could visit five places in the world, where would you go? What are the places of tourist interests in your city?

In the space provided, write the names of the places you come up with.

Travel Destinations

Reading

Read the following description of the Indian hotel industry.

Hotel and Tourism: A Booming Industry

The hotel industry in India has witnessed a huge growth in recent years. It is inextricably linked to the tourism industry. The growth in the Indian tourism industry has fuelled the growth of the Indian hotel industry. The booming economy and increased business opportunities in India have acted as a blessing for Indian hotels. Low-cost airlines have given passengers lots of options. The 'Incredible India' destination campaign has also helped in the growth of domestic and international tourism and consequently. the hotel industry.

In recent years, government has taken several steps to boost travel and tourism, which have benefited the hotel industry in India. These include abolishing the inland air travel tax of 15 per cent; reduction in excise duty on aviation turbine fuel to eight per cent; and removal of a number of restrictions on outbound chartered flights, including those relating to frequency and size of aircraft. The government's recent decision to treat convention centres as part of core infrastructure, allowing the government to provide critical funding for the large capital investment that may be required has also increased the demand for hotel rooms.

The opening up of the aviation industry in India has plenty of opportunities for the hotel industry airlines transport 80 per cent of international arrivals. The government's decision to substantially upgrade 28 regional airports in smaller towns and the privatization and expansion of Delhi and Mumbai airports will improve the business prospects of the hotel industry in India. Substantial investments in tourism infrastructure are essential for the Indian hotel industry to achieve its potential. The upgrading of national highways connecting various parts of India has also opened up new avenues for the development of budget hotels in India.

According to a report, the hotel industry in India currently has 1,10,000 rooms and there is a shortage of 1,50,000 rooms, fuelling rising hotel room rates across India. According to estimates, demand is going to exceed supply by at least 100 per cent over the next two years. With the demand-supply disparity, hotel rates in India are likely to rise by 25 per cent annually and occupancy will go up by 80 per cent over the next two years. This will affect the competitiveness of India as a cost-effective tourist destination.

To overcome this shortage, the Indian hotel industry is adding about 60,000 quality rooms currently in different stages of planning and development, which should be ready by 2012. The hotel Industry in India is also set to get a boost with Delhi hosting the 2010 Commonwealth Games. The government has approved 300 hotel projects, nearly half of which are in the luxury range. The future scenario for the Indian hotel industry looks extremely bright. It is expected that the budget and mid-market hotel segments will witness phenomenal growth and expansion while the luxury segment will continue to perform extremely well over the next few years.

(Adapted from an article in *www.iloveindia.com*)

Essential Vocabulary

Table 3.1 Meanings of Common Words

WORD	MEANING
Inextricably	Cannot be removed
Upgrading	Raising in standard
Abolishing	Removing
Disparity	Gap, difference
Substantial	Significant

Exercise 1

Fill in the blanks with the words given above:

i. There is a big _____________ between the five star and budget hotels.
ii. There is a demand for the _____________ of duty on luxury leather goods.
iii. The airline will be _____________ some of its passengers to the first class.
iv. Tourism is _____________ linked to good transport facilities.

Exercise 2

Answer the following in brief:

i. What are the causes for the boom in the tourism industry in India?

____

____

____

____

ii. What is 'Incredible India'?

____

____

____

____

iii. What role does the aviation industry play in developing tourism?

____

____

____

____

iv. Describe the steps taken by the government to boost tourism in India.

____

____

____

____

Exercise 3
Match the following:

i.	Aviation industry in India	a.	15%
ii.	Hotel rates in India are likely to rise	b.	60,000
iii.	Abolishing of inland air travel tax	c.	Transport 80% of international arrivals
iv.	Number of quality rooms that the Indian hotel industry is adding	d.	25%

REAL-LIFE READS

Hotel Pamphlets

Pre-reading Activity
Find out significant details about the beach resorts in your area. Discuss their features in groups. After your discussion, note down at least three such details in the space given below.

Reading
The following are descriptions of hotels which you might find in pamphlets. Read through them carefully.

Pamphlets

La Residence Hotel and Spa

Location: City Centre, Puducherry
Endowed with opulence and warmth, this former residence of the French colonial governor has been painstakingly restored and refashioned into an exceptionally designed hotel. Its distinctive bowed facade, long horizontal lines and nautical flourishes are hallmarks of the 1930s Streamline Moderne School of art-deco architecture. The airport is 27 kilometres away.
Facilities: 122 rooms and suites. Two restaurants, bar, 24-hour room service, shops, art gallery, safe deposit boxes, business centre, babysitting, inter-connecting and non-smoking rooms.
Superior Rooms: Air-conditioning, TV, wi-fi, minibar, tea, coffee and safe.
Sports and Leisure: Outdoor pool, fitness room, spa, sauna, jacuzzi, massage, billiard room and tennis court.
Check-in: 14:00 hours
Check-out: 12:00 hours

Pamphlets

Ana Manna

Location: M.G. Road, Cochin.

This hotel incorporates the very essence of Vietnamese hospitality and all the comforts of a modern resort. Set amidst almost three hectares of tropical parkland, the Ana Manna Hotel has an enviable location fronting a 400-metre white sand beach and a picturesque countryside. The airport is 35 kilometres away.

Facilities: 58 rooms and suites. Two restaurants, bar, 24-hour room service, shop, business centre, children's activities, babysitting, inter-connecting and non-smoking rooms.

Deluxe rooms: Private balcony, air-conditioning, TV, DVD, wi-fi, minibar, tea and coffee, and safe.

Beach villas: These rooms, located close to the beach, are much larger and have a separate bedroom and sun terrace.

Sports and leisure: Outdoor pool, fitness centre, spa, sauna, steam bath and massage.

Check-in: 14:00 hours

Check-out: 12:00 hours

Pamphlets

Life Heritage Resort

Location: KK Road, Thiruvananthapuram

This resort is situated right on the banks of the Karamana River, only a few steps from the charming town, Thiruvananthapuram, where merchants once traded precious goods and left traces of their many different cultures. It offers guests a sweeping view of tranquil river life and is a short drive from the beautiful beaches. The airport is 35 kilometres away.

Facilities: 54 rooms and suites. Two restaurants, bar, 24-hour room service, shops, beauty salon, safe deposit boxes, business centre, library, babysitting, inter-connecting and non-smoking rooms.

Superior rooms: The rooms overlook the gardens. Air-conditioning, ceiling fan, TV, data ports, minibar, tea and coffee, and safe.

Sports and leisure: Outdoor pool, spa, sauna, massage, biking and kalaripayattu.

Check-in: 14:00 hours

Check-out: 12:00 hours

Pamphlets

The Golden Palm Resort

Location: Panaji beach, Goa.

With a simple design and down-to-earth service, The Golden Palm Resort is an all-pool villa style resort that provides a chic atmosphere of unmatched relaxed luxury. The resort has an unmistakable identity that is inspired by the rich local culture and its stunning location on the white sands of the famed Central Coast. The Goa International Airport is 10 kilometers away.

Facilities: 100 villas, restaurant, bar, 24-hour room service, shop, safe deposit boxes, business centre, library, children's activities, babysitting and non-smoking villas.
One-bedroom villas: TV, DVD, iPod docking station, wi-fi, minibar, tea and coffee, and safe.
Pool villas: Each of these villas has a courtyard entrance and a private pool.
Sports and leisure: Outdoor pools, fitness centre, spa, sauna, steam bath, massage, tennis courts, a badminton and a basketball court.
Check-in: 14:00 hours
Check-out: 12:00 hours

Exercise 1
Answer the following questions.

i. Mention a few leisure activities offered by the resorts.

____

____

____

____

ii. What can one find in a superior room?

____

____

____

____

iii. Which resort offers babysitting facilities?

____

iv. Which hotel claims to have an art deco style of architecture?

____

WRITING

Curriculum Vitae

A curriculum vitae (CV) is defined as a written document required for applying to graduate or professional programmes, for employment with national and international firms, or when promoting oneself within professional and academic fields. A CV is also known as a résumé.

Here is a sample outline of a basic CV. Fill in the relevant details about yourself.

Curriculum Vitae

Name:
Address:
Telephone:
E-mail:
Nationality:
Date of birth:
Employment to date:
Education/Qualifications:
Skills:
Interests:
References:

Discussion

Here are a few other elements which you might want to include in your CV. Discuss what you would write in these sections, with your partner and put down a few points here.

Career goals: ______________________________

Industry exposure: ______________________________

Career highlights: ______________________________

Exercise 1

It's very important to know how to format your résumé to make it look presentable and reader-friendly. Look at the following format and then create your own format in the space given. You can retain, remove or change elements of this format for your résumé.

Name

E-mail: ____________; *Mobile:* ______________

____

Career Goals:

- ______________________________
- ______________________________
- ______________________________

Employment to Date

____

____

____

Education/Qualifications

Internships and Part-time Assignments

Skills

Hobbies and Interests

Personal Details

References available on request.

Your Résumé (formatted):

What is a Cover Letter?

A cover letter is a letter that you send accompanying your CV when you apply for a job, either advertised, or when you are sending an unsolicited application.

Remember:
Most employers read the cover letter first and are likely to look at your CV only if your letter grabs their attention.

Guidelines for Writing a Cover Letter

- To address someone whose name you do not know, you can use 'Dear Sir' or 'Dear Madam'.
- To address someone by name, use their title and surname, for example, 'Dear Dr Rajam'.
- Restrict yourself to one page.
- Type your letter on a computer. Do not write it by hand.
- Make sure it takes one minute or less to read your letter.
- Use plain, neutral-coloured paper without graphics or designs.
- Divide your letter into three parts, with plenty of blank space at the top and the bottom, and along each margin. Use an introduction of a couple of sentences, a middle part of several sentences or bulleted points, and a one or two-sentence conclusion.
- E-mail or post your cover letter and résumé. Nowadays, most employers prefer e-mail. A few job ads ask you to fax your letter and résumé.
- Don't use the following phrases that may first come to mind for a cover letter: 'I am writing to', 'as you can see on my résumé', 'as I have already stated' and 'please don't hesitate to call me'. They waste space because they give no information about you.
- Use spellcheck and grammar check. Employers notice errors in your cover letter more than anywhere else. Even for jobs that do not require writing, employers tend to draw unfavourable conclusions about your work from such errors.
- Use active voice, not passive. Set your word-processing grammar check to check for passive voice. For example, say 'I completed this challenging task' (active), not 'This challenging task was completed by me' (passive).
- End with 'Yours sincerely' if you have addressed the person by their name, and 'Yours faithfully' if you have used 'Dear Sir/Madam'.

Responding to a Job Advertisement

Given below is a job advertisement in a leading newspaper. Write a letter of response, stating that you are including your CV with the cover letter.

Advertisements

Hotel Regent

We are recruiting suitable people for the position of a travel desk executive:
Duties will include:

- Receiving guests at the airport and escorting them to the hotel
- Organizing and escorting coach excursions to tourist attractions

Candidates should be able to:

- Respond to guests' questions and handle their problems
- Assist guests who cannot speak the local language
- Be on call 24 hours to deal with emergencies

Please apply in writing, enclosing your CV, to Ranjit George at rj2001@gmail.com

Your response:

PRONUNCIATION PRACTICE

Percentages

Pronounce the following words:

Four per cent	Twenty-four per cent	Sixty-three per cent
Twelve per cent	Forty-five per cent	Seventy-one per cent
Eighteen per cent	Fifty-nine per cent	Ninety-nine per cent

4

IN THE ELEVATOR

Situation
- Handling guests' luggage

Language Focus
- Idiomatic expressions and phrases
- Strategies of communication

Reading Comprehension
- Elevator etiquette

Grammar Bin
- Using *if*

Real-life Reads
- Restaurant reviews

Speaking
- Presentations

Writing
- Letter to the editor

Workplace Skills
- Basics of etiquette

Pronunciation Practice
- Brands
- Types of luggage

SITUATION

Handling Guests' Luggage

In the three following conversations, you will find how important it is to properly handle the guests' luggage. Though retrieving a guest's delayed luggage from the airport is rarely done by hotels, some do this as a special favour to their guests. Read and practise the conversations.

Conversation 1

Receptionist: Good morning, sir.
Guest: Hi, I'm Praveen Thakur from Indore. I have a reservation from 23rd through the 25th.
Receptionist: That's right. Welcome sir, your room is ready.
Guest: Thank you.
Receptionist: Do you have any luggage, sir?
Guest: Yes, I do, these three bags, with Jet Airways tags.
Receptionist: Certainly, sir. The porter will deliver your luggage to your room, and here's your key. You are in Room 554.
Guest: Thank you.
Receptionist: You're welcome, sir. Have a pleasant stay with us.

Conversation 2

Porter: Can I help you with your luggage, sir?
Guest: Yes please, I think I need a hand. Those two grey bags are mine.
Porter: Certainly, sir. This way please. The lift is just over there. Shall I take your laptop bag too?
Guest: No, thank you.
Porter: Here you are, sir, Room 321.
Guest: Thank you, and here's something for you.
Porter: Thank you very much, sir. I hope you enjoy your stay with us.

Conversation 3

Reception: Good evening. Reception. How may I help you?
Guest: Hi, I checked into Room 233 last evening. My luggage hasn't arrived yet from the airport although they said it would reach me this morning.
Reception: Did you give them our address, sir?
Guest: Yes, I did.
Receptionist: May I have the airline details and the reference number for the luggage, please?
Guest: Sure, it's LH 4563; and the reference number is FRALH 56889.
Receptionist: Thank you, sir. We'll follow it up with the airport authorities. May we get back to you in 30 minutes?

LANGUAGE FOCUS

Idiomatic Expressions and Phrases

The expression 'to need a hand' means to require some help. Consider some more 'hand'-related idioms:

i. **To be good with one's hands:** To be skillful at making or doing things with one's hands.
ii. **Get your hands off somebody or something:** Not to touch somebody or something
iii. **To have one's hands full:** To be very occupied.
iv. **To hand something to somebody on a platter:** To give something to somebody without the person concerned making any effort.
v. **To lay your hands on somebody:** To catch somebody that you are annoyed with
vi. **To play into somebody's hands:** To do exactly what one's enemy or opponent wants
vii. **Hand-me-down:** Cast-off
viii. **To change hands:** For something to pass to a different
ix. **To give someone a big hand:** To applaud someone
x. **To bite the hand that feeds one:** To harm someone who has helped or supported
xi. **In someone's hands:** To be in complete control of someone
xii. **Hands on:** Doing something rather than just talking about it
xiii. **To go to hell in a hand basket:** (British English = to go to the dogs) To get into a very bad situation
xiv. **Hand-picked:** Carefully chosen for a specific purpose

Exercise 1

Fill in the blanks using idioms from the above list:

i. The course is ________________ and not just descriptive. They'll actually train you to cook.
ii. There are two weddings and a conference in the hotel today, our staff's ________________.
iii. The speech was very good and the audience gave her________________.
iv. With three children and a job, Susanna's ________________.
v. The hotel has an excellent staff, all of whom are ________________ by the owner of the place.

Strategies of Communication

Choose the best response to the statements in the first column, from the statements in the second:

i.	I would like to make an appointment.	No, it didn't work out. Saturday would be perfectly fine. What a mess her office was in! She's expected this afternoon. I'll put you through our engineer. When would you like to have our next appointment? You've been cancelling too many appointments. The meeting turned out to be a fiasco. Would Friday be ok?
ii.	I'm afraid it can't take place on Monday.	
iii.	Could we possibly meet on Thursday or Saturday?	
iv.	Has the new desk clerk joined?	

READING COMPREHENSION

Elevator Etiquette

Pre-reading Activity
Did you ever have any trouble with the elevator in your hotel? Share your experience with the class.

Reading
Read the following extract carefully.

Elevator Etiquette

An elevator can be an uncomfortable environment when the riders do not observe the basic rules of common courtesy. As always, follow a basic common sense rule: when you are not sure about how to behave, it is best to treat others as you would wish to be treated.

There are three separate components to elevator etiquette: boarding, riding the elevator and getting out (disembarking). Many a time, we find people taking the elevator for just a floor or two. This is rude and causes inconvenience to those who need to go up several floors, are carrying heavy packages or are with small children.

Boarding etiquette dictates that you should wait until everyone who is getting off has left the elevator before you step inside. People who carry lots of luggage or are travelling in a big group, should wait for an empty elevator. Often we find people ignoring this golden rule of etiquette and causing plenty of discomfort to others. The same rule applies if one is sick, particularly if carrying an infectious disease.

While in an elevator, one should not eat, smoke or talk on the cellphone. Many people prefer to ride an elevator in silence, so we must do our best to respect their privacy and give them space. Again, it is important to step aside for people getting off the elevator, and to avoid blocking the door when the elevator stops.

It is also preferable to call out 'I'm going off the floor' in case you find the elevator too crowded for comfort. That way, you can avoid confusion and jostling at the door.

Remember, elevators are meant for everyone's comfort. A little consideration for your fellow travellers goes a long way in making your ride pleasant and comfortable.

(Adapted from an article on www.wisegeek.com)

Exercise 1
Answer the following in one or two sentences:

i. What is 'the common sense rule' the writer talks about?

____

____

____

____

ii. What is the 'going off the floor' alert the writer refers to?

____

____

____

____

iii. What does the writer advise those who carry heavy luggage?

____

____

____

____

iv. What are the do's and don'ts to observe in elevators?

____

____

____

____

Exercise 2

Fill in the blanks using words from the above passage:

i. The three separate components to elevator etiquette are ____________, ____________ and ____________.
ii. While in an elevator, one should not ____________, ____________ or talk on the ____________.
iii. If we are sick, we should wait for ____________ elevator.

GRAMMAR BIN

Using 'If'

The word *if* implies a condition, and when followed by *be*, the sentence suggests that one situation is dependent on another situation or a person. Conditional sentences, thus, are used to express that the action in the main clause (without *if*) can only take place if a certain condition (in the clause with *if*) is fulfilled. Consider the following sentences:

- If you are carrying heavy packages or travelling with a big group, you should wait for an empty elevator.
- If you are only travelling one or two floors, taking the stairs is more polite, unless you are disabled.
- If you are trapped in the back of a crowded elevator and you need to get off, call out 'my floor' to alert other riders.
- If you aren't certain about whether or not a behaviour is appropriate in an elevator, ask yourself how comfortable you would be if someone else in the elevator did it first.

Exercise 1

Complete the following sentences using the expressions given in the box:

> If there's an earthquake
> If it weren't for the timely intervention by the manager
> If I had Johnny's phone number
> If they get married
> If it weren't for his brother's support

i. ________________, they'll have to find their own place to live.
ii. ________________, this problem would have become serious.
iii. ________________, Shyam wouldn't have got the job.
iv. ________________, avoid the use of the elevator.
v. ________________, I would have contacted him today.

REAL-LIFE READS

Restaurant Reviews

Read the following restaurant reviews.

Reviews

Wrapped Up: 4/5

'I'll have a sandwich and coffee to go, please. Thanks'. And you're off. The gourmet upmarket delicatessen, Wrapped Up, has everything you need. Quick and efficient, there are lots of pre-packed meals, gourmet salads as well as sweet and savoury Asian and Western style snacks to choose from as you are heading out the door.

Twenty Four Hours Parking: Available

Asian Kitchen: 4/5

Make your taste buds tingle with East Asian Cuisine. Here at Asian Kitchen, guests can experience the fun of an interactive live kitchen, and the difference that personalized and intuitive service can make.

Cuisine: Pan-Asian

Opening Hours: 11:30 am–11:45 pm

Atmosphere: Interactive Kitchen

Parking: Available

Kangan: 5/5

Modern, stylish and with a mix of tradition, Kangan is a visually appealing and inviting contemporary Indian restaurant showcasing an impressive tandoor show kitchen, replete with private rooms. In keeping with India's deep rooted, age old culture, the delectable and aromatic sample plates and platters entice and encourage family style dining.

Cuisine: Indian

Opening Hours: 7:00 pm–12:00 am

Phone: +91 22 61470000

Atmosphere: Cosy, relaxed, vibrant

Setting: Table and booth seating and 2 private dining rooms

Sky Grill: 3.5/5

Sky Grill specializes in authentic, delicious, barbecue specialties. It's an ideal place for a family gathering or for barbeque connoisseurs. Also on the menu: tasty concoctions of Indian and international liquors.

Cuisine: Barbeque

Dress Code: Casual

Opening Hours: 7:00 pm–11:45 pm on weekends only

Atmosphere: Al Fresco dining

Setting: Poolside

Prego: 4.5/5

Casual and comfortable, Prego is the perfect place to bring the whole family. Its lively colourful décor, enhanced by the aromas of fresh bread and pizza baking in the wood-fired oven, entice one to enter and join in the warm and friendly atmosphere.

Opening Hours: 12:00 pm–12:00 am

Lunch: 12:00 pm–3:00 pm

Happy Hour: 5:00 pm–7:00 pm

Dinner: 7:00 pm–12:00 am

Phone: +91 22 61470000

Atmosphere: Fun, lively, casual

Setting: Upscale trattoria with indoor and outdoor dining

Exercise 1

Write the name of the restaurant being referred to in the following sentences:

i. This restaurant has a rating of 3.5: ____________________

ii. This is an upscale trattoria: ____________________

iii. This restaurant has a personalized and intuitive service: ____________________

Exercise 2

Match the name of the restaurant with the descriptions:

i.	Wrapped up	a.	Colourful decor
ii.	Prego	b.	Gourmet take away
iii.	Asian Kitchen	c.	Barbecue specialties
iv.	Kangan	d.	Two private dining rooms
v.	Sky Grill	e.	Interactive kitchen

Exercise 3

Use the following words in sentences of your own:

i. Décor: ____________________

ii. Upscale: ____________________

iii. Aromas: ____________________

iv. Gourmet: ____________________

v. Connoisseurs: ____________________

The culture of reviewing food and restaurants is well-established in our society. To learn more about this art, visit:

http://en.wikipedia.org/wiki/Food_critic

http://www.guardian.co.uk/lifeandstyle/wordofmouth/2008/mar/20/levycritics

Culture

SPEAKING

Presentations

1. Make a verbal presentation before your class on the décor and setting of any two restaurants of a hotel. Compare the two.

STUDENT'S NOTES

2. Make a presentation on the variety of desserts made in your hotel. Discuss the ingredients used in them.

STUDENT'S NOTES

WRITING

Letter to the Editor

A restaurant critic has reviewed your restaurant in a leading magazine, where he has written unfavourably about the food and atmosphere of the place. Write a letter to the editor of the magazine defending your restaurant.

WORKPLACE SKILLS

Basics of Etiquette

Pre-reading Activity

Have you ever attended a workshop/training on hotel etiquettes? What did you learn there? Discuss in groups.

Reading

Read the following extract from the book *English for Careers* on general etiquettes in corporate situations:

Basics of Etiquette

Whether you go on to work in a non-profit organization or a multinational corporation or any other professional space, you will spend a lot of time in close proximity to people. Etiquette is the set of rules that should govern your conduct. These include socially acceptable behaviour, codes of conduct or procedures prescribed by any authority in the social/official context and practices prescribed by social convention. How you present yourself and treat your co-workers in the business world speaks volumes about you. It's sometimes not what you say, but how you say it that counts. In a meeting, your careful navigation across hierarchies will maintain your professional image.

You might wonder why we need to follow rules of etiquette. What is wrong with expressing your real impression about someone? Why is it wrong and even dangerous to express your dislike or scorn for someone openly? There are several reasons. It helps you avoid needless negative confrontation and unhealthy politics. Confrontations usually cause bad blood between people.

This tends to cause tension between people and stress, hindering efficiency. Politics often pits people against each other, also adversely affecting work. Following the rules of etiquette helps people to be organized and efficient, to communicate effectively and to be socially aware and responsible workers.

At a very basic level, etiquette, as with all other interpersonal skills, is about building relationships. No rules of communication will have the desired effect if you forget the human touch. How do you do that? Do not be eager to show off the flagrant aspects of your personality when you join an organization. Instead, understand and adjust to your surroundings. These are a few points to note when you join your first job.

Meetings, Conferences and Social Gatherings

Your social skills are always open for analysis when you are attending or hosting meetings, conferences or unofficial social gatherings. In all these occasions, your attitude and your etiquette play a vital role in bridging or breaking business relations. Every country will have its standard norms for all these occasions. It is essential for you to be aware of these norms before you start working.

Dressing Etiquette

How you dress is an important factor in any business relationship. Appearance and how one carries oneself are the first things that are noticed when a person walks into the room. Proper attire is likely to inspire confidence and respect in the people you deal with. You should wear clean, comfortable, fitted and ironed clothes. Avoid gaudy colours and provocative attire.

For official gatherings, men may opt for formal suits or blazers with a tie, or a full-sleeved formal shirt. Your hair should be neatly groomed. Men should be shaved. Apply aftershave, but be careful that it isn't too loud. The tie should be double-knotted. The suit, shirt, tie and shoes should be coordinated. And remember, never wear sneakers with formal attire!

Women can wear pant suits, *salwar kameez* or *saris* in the workplace. The office environment is more of a deciding factor for women than men in the choice of attire. Some workplaces, where you are required to deal with foreign clients or associates, insist on Western formal wear. In some offices, you might be allowed to wear skirts and even jeans. Others might insist on Indian attire. Women should also be careful that their jewellery and shoes are coordinated with their attire.

Exercise 1

Answer the following in brief:

i. Why does the writer advise us to control our feelings and emotions in an office environment?

____

____

____

____

ii. What is the writer's attitude towards dress code for women in workplaces?

____

____

____

____

iii. What are the skills necessary for a business meeting?

____

____

____

____

Exercise 2

Complete the following passage by using the appropriate expressions given in the list below:

To impress	Be attentive and enthusiastic	Make eye contact
With a smile	Make value judgements	

The Etiquette Table

Remember, the first impression is the most lasting. So, take care how you present yourself.

i. Maintain correct posture—stand straight, ______________, turn towards people when they are speaking.

ii. Greet your co-workers ______________ in the morning. When meeting someone for the first time, be sure to shake hands palm to palm with gentle firmness.

iiii. Be patient with other people and their ways even if you don't agree with them.

iv. Dress ______________ by following your office dress code.

v. Be organized. Carry only what you require and keep your work desk clean.

vi Don't ______________ —talk to the maintenance staff members and remember to thank them for their efforts.

vii. Be kind and courteous to all. Remember that everyone is equal, there is no room for partiality.

viii. Never be late—try to be early for work, a little extra time to arrange your schedule is always welcome.

ix. One way of winning people over is by doing your work well. ______________ about your work.

Dictionary Work

Find out the meanings of the following words. Work in pairs:

- Proximity
- Hierarchies
- Flagrant
- Confrontations
- Bad blood
- Provocative

PRONUNCIATION

Practise the pronunciation of the following words:

Brands	*Types of Luggage*
Atlantic	Backpack
American Tourister	Carrier bag
Altman	Fanny pack
Boyt	Duffel bag
Delsey	Brief case
High Sierra	Attaché case
Samsonite	Rucksack
Skyway	
Travelpro	
Tumi	
Victorinox Swiss Army	
V.I.P.	

5

Responding to Enquiries After Checking In

Situation
- Facilitating the guests' comfort in their rooms

Real-life Reads
- Reading a brochure

Reading
- Room service

Speaking
- The guest and the housekeeper

Vocabulary
- Types of bathroom accessories
- Quality of food

Grammar Bin
- Countable and uncountable nouns
- Singular and plural nouns

Writing
- Memorandum

Workplace Skills
- Entrepreneurship

Pronunciation Practice
- Items in a hotel

SITUATION

Facilitating the Guests' Comfort in Their Rooms

A guest may, more often than not, enquire about facilities which are very obvious and easily visible. However, the key to the situation is to patiently and politely respond to all queries. Read and practise the following conversation to help you understand this better:

Housekeeper: Housekeeping. Good afternoon, how may I help you?
Guest: Hi. I need some extra towels. Could you arrange for some?
Housekeeper: Certainly, sir.
Guest: And I can't find the light switch in the bathroom.
Housekeeper: The light switch is right next to the mirror, sir.
Guest: Yes, it's here. And please could you send me a hair dryer?
Housekeeper: The dryer is in the drawer of the dressing table, sir.
Guest: I see. And can I have a bathrobe?
Housekeeper: There should be a bathrobe in the bedroom cupboard, sir.
Guest: Fine. And where can I find bathroom slippers?
Housekeeper: You'll find a pair under the wash basin, sir.
Guest: Alright, thank you so much.
Housekeeper: You're welcome, sir. Would there be anything else?
Guest: Yes, I would like to have some extra coffee sachets after an hour or so.
Housekeeper: Certainly, sir. I'll have them sent up your room by 2 pm.

Exercise 1

Complete the following sentences using the words from the above conversation:

i. The ________________ is in the dressing table drawer.
ii. The ________________ is next to the bathroom mirror.
iii. The ________________ is in the bedroom cupboard.
iv. ________________ will be sent up by 2 pm.
v. You can find the ________________ under the wash basin.

REAL-LIFE READS

Reading a Brochure

Go through the following hotel brochure.

Brochure

Hotel Poem

- Fifty-five rooms +11 suites with full air conditioning
- Eleven suites: four-poster bed, luxury bathroom with jacuzzi
- Twenty-five double rooms: king-size bed, luxury bathroom
- Eleven double rooms: twin beds, en-suite bathroom, TV
- Eight single rooms: shower only, TV
- Personal safe available
- All rooms are wi-fi connected
- Fax, computers, secretarial services available in the business centre

Exercise 1

Fill in the blanks using the information provided in the brochure:

In the Hotel Poem:

i. There are showers in ________________ rooms only.
ii. ________________ rooms are wi-fi connected.
iii. ________________ have jacuzzi.
iv. ________________ have king-size beds.
v. Eleven double rooms have ________________ beds.
vi. Secretarial services are available in the ________________.

READING COMPREHENSION

Room Service

Pre-reading Activity

What are the items on the room service menu of your hotel? List a few here.

____

____

____

____

____

____

____

Reading

Now read the following passage on room service.

Room Service Takes a New Turn

Room service appeals to guests for many reasons: After a long day of meetings, you can unwind with your meal without having to get dressed for dinner; if you are travelling by yourself, you don't have to deal with a table for one in the dining room.

Many top chefs who have opened restaurants within hotels are now tinkering with the room-service menu or even handling all the food and beverage operations at the property—from the restaurant to the lounges to in-room dining. Chefs are also adding their own gourmet spin to traditional room-service items like burgers and salads, as well as expanding in-room menus with dishes from the onsite restaurant. As a result, guests will find that room service is no longer an afterthought but an integral component of the overall food-and-beverage picture.

Food and beverage directors are noticing that guests, in their quest for healthier eating, are asking more detailed questions about the cuisine: Where does it come from? How is it prepared? What's the portion size? What's the calorie count?

Despite the fact that healthy dishes are on the rise, another clear emerging trend is renewed enthusiasm for comfort food. One of the obvious reasons why: Comfort food reminds people of home and family. These dishes also tend to be filling, quick to prepare and on the less expensive side—a definite advantage nowadays. Since everyone is being extra careful with their finances, it's nice to be a little indulgent—even if it's just via an order of mac 'n' cheese.

At some places, you will find breakfast treats like New England crab cakes Benedict and all-day offerings like clam chowder, Cuban pork sandwiches with sweet-potato fries and Maine lobster pot pie with a flaky crust. Other hotels offer BBQ short ribs and lobster, fill the surf-and-turf dumplings, while the InterContinental Mark Hopkins in San Francisco serves up shepherd's pie and meat loaf.

(Adapted from an article by Jill Fergus on *www.executivetravelmagazine.com*)

Exercise 1

Answer the following questions.

i. What accounts for the appeal of room service dining?

____

____

____

____

____

ii. How are top chefs tinkering with the room service menu of hotels?

iii. What is comfort food?

iv. What are the questions that guests ask these days?

Exercise 2

Some words from the passage are given below, along with their meanings. Make sentences with these words:

i. **Unwind:** relax

ii. **Tinkering:** playing with, considering

iii. **Afterthought:** something which is not so significant

iv. **Purveyor:** one who furnishes provisions, especially food

SPEAKING

The Guest and the Housekeeper

You are the housekeeper of a luxury hotel. A guest orders a film DVD over the phone. Enact the situation.

VOCABULARY

Types of Bathroom Accessories

Look at the pictures of these two bathrooms. Make a list of the items you see in the space given below:

____

____

____

____

Attributes of Food

Foods like burgers, pizzas, hot dogs and curries are preferred hot. Similarly, we like chilled beer, chilled Coke, seasoned stew (stew with added herbs, salts, spices) and so on.

Exercise 1

Given below is a list of food items. Match their respective qualities from the other column. Discuss your answers with your partner.

SL. NO.	FOOD	ATTRIBUTE
i.	Rice	Steamed
ii.	Fries	Brown
iii.	Fish	Deep fried

SL. NO.	FOOD	ATTRIBUTE
iv.	Eggs	Scrambled
v.	Pizza	Strong, black
vi.	Coffee	With mayo
vii.	Salad	With maple syrup
viii.	Salmon paté	With mustard-chive dressing
ix.	Pancake	Salt and pepper

GRAMMAR BIN

Countable and Uncountable Nouns

Nouns can be either countable or uncountable. Countable nouns are those which have the word *a/an* before them or can be used in the plural. Uncountable nouns are not used with *a/an* or in the plural.

Example of countable noun: There are three *children*, two *cars* and *a driver*.

Example of an uncountable noun: I went out to get some fresh *air*.

The plural of news *is* news.

Remember!

Given below is a list of some uncountable nouns:

Accommodation
Advice
Assistance
Baggage
Cash
Conduct
Cutlery
Dirt
Employment
Equipment
Furniture
Health
Housing
Information
Leisure
Luck
Machinery
Money
Music
News
Nonsense
Parking
Pay
Permission
Photography
Poetry
Pollution
Publicity
Score
Research
Rubbish
Scenery
Shopping
Sunshine
Transport
Violence
Weather

Look at the following examples which show incorrect usage of plurals:

- She has a good collection of antique furnitures. (**Correct:** furniture)
- He always seeks my advices. (**Correct:** advice)

- This book has some excellent informations. (**Correct:** information)
- The news are true. (**Correct:** is)
- The girl has golden hairs. (**Correct:** hair)

Exercise 1

Now read the following sentences and rewrite them correctly:

i. The guests have ordered fruits.

____

ii. The office has ordered four scores pencils for use.

____

iii. Twenty miles are a long distance.

____

iv. The United States have a big navy.

____

v. In this town, most houses are made of stones, but in the next town, bricks are more common.

____

vi. We need some more woods for construction.

____

vii. My researches prove that I am right.

____

viii. She has loads of charms.

____

ix. Don't waste your talents.

____

x. Carry lots of warm clothings to Scotland.

____

Singular and Plural Verb Forms

- *If you use a plural noun, you must use a plural verb.*
- *The verb must 'agree' with the noun.*

Remember!

Exercise 1

Identify the correct sentence in each pair:

1. a. There are many room on this floor.
   b. There are many rooms on this floor.
2. a. Many NGO provides a great deal of help to these workers.
   b. Many NGOs provide a great deal of help to these workers.

Plural Nouns

We use a plural noun with:

- Plural verbs: *are, were, have, do*, etc.
  We *are* nine brothers.
  They *do* not go home during vacations.
- Numbers greater than one.
  10 tables, 30 waiters, etc.
- Many.
  There are many chefs in this restaurant.

Singular Nouns

We use a singular noun with:

- Singular verbs: is, was, has, does, etc.
  He *is* a waiter.
  She *has* a degree in hotel management.
- A/an or one.
  A manager, an oven, one man, etc.

Exercise 2

Fill in the blanks using the appropriate form of the verbs given in the brackets:

i. Catering ________________ (be) a popular career choice.
ii. A hotel management course ________________ (cost) approximately ₹2,00,000 at this institute.
iii. The staff of this hotel ________________ (be) paid high salaries.
iv. The hotel's earnings ________________ (has) increased over the last three years.
v. The premises of the hotel ________________ (be) well-maintained.

WRITING

Memorandum

A memorandum or memo is a brief note sent by the highest-ranking person in an office/organization to the staff members. It is meant only for in-house communication and is not for public circulation.

Exercise 1

As a manager of your hotel, send a memorandum to your staff about an upcoming workshop on interpersonal communication, which your hotel is organizing.

Your memo should consist of the following details about the workshop:

- Date/day and venue
- Information about the speaker
- A briefing about the workshop and its professional significance

Write your memorandum in the following space:

Know more about memoranda at http://www.wisegeek.com/what-is-a-memorandum.htm

Culture

WORKPLACE SKILLS

Entrepreneurship

Pre-reading Activity

Name the major entrepreneurs from India and note them down in the space below. Discuss with your partner why you admire them. Share your answers with the class.

Reading

The passage given here is taken from the book *India: Land of a Billion Entrepreneurs* by Upendra Kachru. Read the passage.

Entrepreneurship: How Do They Get There?

Size and shape do not define entrepreneurship. Entrepreneurship can be found in large enterprises as well as in small and medium enterprises (SMEs); and also in tiny and micro-enterprises. In a world preoccupied with 'bigness', the classification of small and medium units can be misleading. By conservative estimates, entrepreneurial firms in the small and medium sector account for nearly half of India's manufacturing output and nearly 40 per cent of exports. There are over 13 million SMEs, employing over 42 million people. Clearly, the role they play in national development is critical.

I would like to call the entrepreneurs in the small and medium sectors the 'defenders'. They are defenders in more senses than one. Not only do they protect the Indian turf from incursions, but they also play an important role in its development. They are at the heart of the story of India's exciting growth. They are largely responsible for the explosive growth of the middle classes in India and also for creating unbelievable wealth. In the real sense, these small and medium entrepreneurs are the stars of India's irrepressible entrepreneurial spirit. It is their sheer numbers that make India a great entrepreneurial nation.

These 'defenders' have largely been at the vanguard of change. These are people who have had the courage to seek opportunity and accept risk. They form the foundation of India's enormous entrepreneurial ambitions.

There are a number of stories of successful entrepreneurs who fall in the 'defender' category. Amongst these are a class of entrepreneurs who show an unusual passion to win. I call them the 'explorers'. Explorers have been there in every society. In India, most of the explorers have emerged in the last decade. These entrepreneurs have, from ordinary beginnings, turned their enterprises into great enterprises; some of these have become mini-multinationals and some have turned into growth leaders. Some of these are small and some are not as small as one would imagine.

A small Indian company, Hidesign, has built for itself a global consumer brand without having to wait for decades and without investing millions. Its story is highly instructive and impressive. How did it do this? Instead of acquiring strong international brands, Hidesign chose to globally promote its own corporate brand by embracing its 'Indianness'. The brand essence is captured in its tag line: 'Real leather, crafted the forgotten way'.

The foundations of the company were laid in Pondicherry in 1978. It was started by Dilip Kapur, who attended Princeton University and earned a bachelor's and master's degree from there. Then he went on to pursue a Ph.D. in Denver University. During his stay in the United States, he spent a year working for an American company that made and sold handbags. Kapur had grown up in Pondicherry. He returned to India in 1978 and began making leather bags as a hobby, drawing upon what he had learned in the United States.

Hidesign started as a one-man workshop for tanned leather bags and jackets. By 1986, several hundred people were working with him to make and sell bags using vegetable-tanned leather. Hidesign was started in 1990. In 2000, Kapur decided to start his own chain of exclusive boutiques across India. Says Kapur, 'We looked for a distributor but we couldn't find a suitable one. Modern retailing was just starting in India, so we decided to open our own store in Pondicherry. It was successful, so we opened stores in Bangalore and Mumbai and kept growing'.

The company which started as a company to stem the influx of imported high fashion leather goods and promote Indian workmanship now operates its stores in Australia, the United States, Norway, Russia, the United Kingdom, Greece, Sri Lanka, Malaysia, the United Arab Emirates, South Africa and, of course, in India.

Hidesign has an expansive portfolio of leather products including bags for work and travel, accessories and belts focused on the mass luxury segment. Its designs emphasize workmanship and quality. Seventy per cent of the manufacturing is done by hand. This results in beautiful, affordable bags. Hidesign has used the large pool of skilled workers available in India to challenge its Italian peers using traditional production methods long abandoned in developed nations. Kapur says, 'We have the capability to create a product which is very individualistic but does not have to be sold at the high price levels that Europe needs for profitable sales'. So I think we have a special space which we will call affordable luxury'.

The tale of Marico, owned by Harsh Mariwala, a second-tier company in the consumer goods (FMCG) sector, is another interesting story. Harsh was faced with the dilemma of competing with multinational brands to defend his own turf. He decided to attack. Instead of acquiring an international brand, Mariwala used its Indian character to advantage. Unlike Hidesign, which targeted the markets in developed countries, Harsh used a strategy of leveraging on international markets, which have traditions similar to that of India and the Indian diaspora. Over the last three decades, Marico has taken its traditional commodity- driven business in new directions. It has now taken a lead to convert itself into a company entrenched in the 'Beauty and Wellness' space. From a turnover of ₹5 million in 1971, Marico's products and services in hair care, skin care and health foods generated a turnover of about ₹23.9 billion ($475 million) in 2008–09.

Marico's flagship brand is 'Parachute', a well-known producer of coconut-based hair oil. Parachute coconut oil was a market leader in India for many years. Marico realized there was a market for its product in the Middle East and other parts of the world that had large Indian expatriate populations. In the mid-1990s, Marico began its international debut by exporting to neighbouring markets. In the late 1990s, it set up a manufacturing plant in Bangladesh, a country with consumption patterns like those of India. Within a decade, Parachute captured a lion's share of the Bangladesh market. It launched several product and packaging innovations, and extended its range of offerings to include hair creams, gels, moisturizers and treatments, as well as new bottles and individual-use packets. From an India-centric approach to innovation, its model is focused on serving the needs of the local markets.

Today, Parachute is the world's largest packaged coconut oil brand. It has substantial presence in Bangladesh, the Gulf, South Africa and Egypt, and is present in over 25 countries. It competes with global brands like Sunsilk from Unilever and Brylcreem from Sara Lee. In 2007, Marico was one of eight Indian companies included in the *Business Week* list of 100 Asian 'hot-growth' companies and the *Standard & Poor's* list of global challengers. In 2008, Bangladesh Brand Forum ranked Parachute as the sixth most-trusted brand in Bangladesh, ahead of global brands such as Coke, Pepsi, Sony and Samsung. In 2008, *Business Today* rated it as one of India's most innovative companies. The company has indeed come a long way.

Exercise 1

Answer the following questions in one or two sentences:

i. Who are the 'defenders', according to the writer?

____

____

____

____

ii. How did Hidesign make it big?

____

____

____

____

iii. How was Parachute hair oil exported and turned into an international brand?

____

____

____

____

Exercise 2

State whether the following statements are true or false:

i. Hidesign did not want to capitalize on its Indianness. ______________

ii. Marico exported its goods in the not so developed countries. ______________

iii. The headquarter of Hidesign is in Kanpur. ______________

Dictionary Work

Find out the meanings of the following words. Work in pairs.

i. Turf ______________________________

ii. Incursion ______________________________

iii. Flagship ______________________________

iv. Hot growth ______________________________

v. Leveraging ______________________________

vi. Lion's share ______________________________

vii. To come a long way ______________________________

PRONUNCIATION PRACTICE

Items in a Hotel

Pronounce the following words:

Shower	Geyser	Coffee-maker
Hair dryer	Jacuzzi	Suitcase stand
Bath mat	Air-conditioning	Laundry bag

6

Room Service

Situation
- Responding to a room service request
- Apologizing to a guest

Grammar Bin
- Time expressions

Speaking
- Small talk with guests
- Presentation: Your favourite book

Writing
- Letter to the editor

Workplace Skills
- Disaster planning in the workplace

Pronunciation
- Numbers

SITUATION

Responding to a Room Service Request

A guest requests for room service at a hotel. Read and practise the following conversation:

Staff: Good evening. Room service. How can I help you?
Guest: Hi, I'm in 1125. What time do you start dinner?
Staff: At 7.30 pm, sir. However, you could order from the round-the-clock section at any time. Would you like to place your order now?
Guest: Yes. I would like to have one grilled chicken with garlic bread.
Staff: Certainly, sir. Would you like to place an order for a side dish?
Guest: I'm not too sure. What would you suggest?
Staff: How about some bacon?
Guest: No, I don't particularly like bacon. I think I'll go for some cheese.
Staff: Very well, sir. What about some dessert? We've some excellent apple strudel.
Guest: Sounds good. I'll have it.
Staff: May I repeat your order, sir? One grilled chicken with garlic bread, some cheese slices and apple strudel.
Guest: That's right.
Staff: Would you like us to send some extra plates or would the order be for one person, sir?
Guest: Just for myself.
Staff: Thank you, sir. Your dinner will be served by 8 o'clock. Please allow us 20 minutes for service.
Guest: Thank you.

Apologizing to a Guest

A hotel staff member offers his apologies for a mistake made in the order. Read and practise the following conversation:

Staff: Good evening. Room service. How can I help you?
Guest: Hi, I'm at 1101. I just ordered some sausage soup and the waiter delivered tomato soup to me.
Staff: I'm sorry, sir. May we have the soup replaced? It can be served within 10 minutes.
Guest: Please do that.
Staff: Certainly sir. Do accept our apologies for the error.

Exercise 1

The following is the menu of Waterfront restaurant. Read it carefully and then answer the questions given below:

Menu

WATERFRONT

Breakfast

Monday.–Friday. 7:00am–10:00am • Saturday & Sunday
7:30am–10:30am

Please make your selections from separate breakfast room service card

All Day Dining

12:00 pm–9:00 pm

Clam Chowder
Cheddar Ale and Sausage Soup

Grilled Portobello and Eggplant Sandwich
Red Onion, Lemon Hummus and Naan

Soup Selection of the Day
Frisee, Radicchio and Baby Spinach
Traditional Caesar Salad
White Anchovies and Garlic Croutons

Add to any Salad
Grilled Chicken Breast
Grilled Salmon

Desserts
Pineapple Pie
Carrot Bundt Cake
Pecan Balls
Vanilla Ice Cream and Maple Glaze
Chocolate Pudding
Vanilla Whipped Cream
Warm Brown Sugar Cake
Coffee Ice Cream & Caramel Sauce
Roasted Pumpkin Crème Brûlée
Butterscotch Cookies
Indian Pudding
Molasses, Cornmeal and Raisins
Apple Pie, Served Warm with Vanilla Ice Cream

Selection of Ice Creams & Sorbets

A guest orders from room service. Read this conversation and complete the sentences:

Room service: Good afternoon. Room service. Can I help you?
Guest: I would like some light snacks, please. Is ____________
Room service: Yes, sir it is. One Caesar salad. Would that be all, sir?
Guest: Yes, thank you ____________ some spinach soup as well.
Room service: Certainly. So that's ____________ and ____________ And what ____________
Guest: Room 1109.
Room service: Very well, sir. It will take ____________
Guest: About 20 minutes, fine.

Discussion

Enact a telephone conversation between a house guest and a room service staff member. Place an order for desserts from the following menu card. Take turns at role playing.

Menu

Desserts	
Fresh Fruit Salad	₹250
Apple Pie	₹500
Mango Soufflé	₹450
Chocolate Soufflé	₹550
Selection of ice cream	₹350
Gulab jamun (2 pieces)	₹150
Coffee & Tea	
Cappuccino, Espresso	₹150
Hot chocolate	₹180
Herbal tea	₹160
Fresh Juice	
Seasonal (Mango, orange, apple)	₹150

GRAMMAR BIN

Time Expressions

Consider words such as *on, when, till, at, before, during, after, at times, often, at around, earlier* and *by*. These are called time expressions because they help us talk about time.

Exercise 1

Fill in the blanks using *since, ago, in, on at, during, still.*

i. She will see her tutor ________ the evening.
ii. Some people feel depressed ________ the winter season.
iii. Doctors have discussed the issue ________ the beginning of medicine
iv. Several people visited my college ________ Thursday.
v. Most people are well ________ spring and summer.
vi. Our anatomy class usually begins ________ 9 o'clock.
viii. This vaccine was discovered nearly 50 years ________.
viii. The institute placement test will be given ________ November 25 and 27.
ix. The weather is usually warm ________ March.
x. After Christmas vacation, I will see you again ________ January.
xi. This will probably come true ________ the future.
xii. Tanya is ________ in hospital and her husband is going to work.

Exercise 2

Use the following time-related expressions in sentences of your own:

- Three months ago

  ____

- Six days ago

  ____

- Five years ago

  ____

- Half an hour ago

  ____

- In April

  ____

- In 2007

  ____

- Last year

  ____

- Last Monday

  ____

SPEAKING

Small Talk With Guests

Imagine a conversation with a calorie-conscious guest in your hotel. Enact the situation before the class. You may want to include some of these conversation points in the situation:

- 'We believe in looking after the health of our guests, therefore….'
- 'Indian food too can be healthy, which is what our hotel's restaurant is trying to prove by….'
- 'We have a special package for calorie-conscious people, which includes…'

Presentation: Your Favourite Book

Which is your favourite book? Make a verbal presentation on it discussing its significant features. You may want to include some of the following points:

- What you like most about the book
- Other books by the same author
- Why others should read the book

WRITING

Letter to the Editor

Read the following piece:

Article

Energy Drinks: What Lies Beneath

Manufacturers of sports drinks appear to have successfully deceived children and their parents into believing that their products are healthy, according to a study.

Researchers found that children who participated in more sports and vigorous physical activities drank significantly less soda than less active children, but higher levels of sports drinks. Children with higher sports drink consumption also ate more fruits and vegetables, while children with high soda consumption ate less.

Exercise 1

As a chief chef of a major hotel, write a letter to the editor of a leading newspaper responding to the above article. You must include the following points:

- About yourself and your experience in the hotel industry
- Your personal point of view (if you agree/disagree with the article)
- Support from existing research/evidence to substantiate your position

____

____

____

WORKPLACE SKILLS

Disaster Planning in the Workplace

Pre-reading Activity

Make an individual presentation on the importance of customer service relations in the hotel industry. You may want to include some of the following points:

- Customer service is important in any organization, since it is the basic and sometimes the only contact point with customers.
- Good customer relations can make or break an organization in the hospitality sector.
- Good customer service is often the best way to get repeated business from customers.

Reading

Now read the following passage and answer the questions that follow:

When Things Go Way Wrong in Our Workplace

What happens 'When things go way wrong in our workplace'; especially, when most of us have visions of sailing through our careers and retiring with glory—and a gold watch. But today's globally competitive, dog-eat-dog world is more like the rough seas, exposing organizations to corporate equivalents of tsunamis and typhoons. And if an organizational disaster indeed strikes, many corporations these days simply implode and self-destruct under the impact, causing widespread damage and deeply painful consequences.

At the individual level, a corporate storm has the potential to ruin many, many careers and professional lives. If you are in its path, you will not be spared, no matter whether you are a bit player or a major player. Given this brutal reality, we should be open to the idea of a possible career disruption due to office events and must do at least a bare minimum of risk management and disaster-recovery planning, in advance. They will show you why disaster-planning is not just for the disaster-prone and paranoids, but in everyone's interest.

NNA Corp. has always been your top customer. It is an MNC with an office in practically every street corner in the world and it is a matter of pride that you have them in your client list. Not only that, every year the account is getting larger and larger with you poaching projects from your rivals. In fact, your company dedicates a separate department (including 'hot line' phones) to mollycoddle NNA. Then one day you hear the news that your big rival has trumped you and stolen the NNA account from you—lock, stock and barrel. The 'unhappenable' has happened. Within a few days, you find yourself sitting squarely on the 'bench', waiting for the next assignment.

You work for Fizz Bottled Drinks Inc. Your company has ambitious plans of entering and capturing the juice-drink market. You and your colleagues in research and development labour for months and come up with formulae for several juice-drink flavours. The first such product—called Mang-Jooz, a mango drink, is test-marketed in several parts of the country and based on the positive marketing results, it is introduced nationwide, with celebrity brand ambassadors and promo videos and all that jazz. But within a month, the bubble bursts and Mang-Jooz turns out to be one of the biggest fiascos in the industry. After enormous losses, Fizz not only gives up on the mango drink, but also puts the entire line of juice-drinks follow-products in permanent cold storage. You were counting on the success of this line of products to vault you into higher orbit. But, now you are re-assigned to an insignificant job of doing minor chemistry experiments in a jungle of test tubes and round-bottomed flasks. Your programme manager was not so lucky. He got transferred to your Antarctica office or something like that.

You work in AB Mutual Funds Company. You earned huge bonuses and incentive pay just last year when the entire country was hungrily grabbing up shares of your mutual funds. But this year, with the global economic downturn, there are no takers for your mutual funds even if you gave it to them for free (well, almost). Stock trading activity has come to a crawl and your company makes a tough decision to close its Kolkata office and lay-off the entire staff—including you.

There are some things in common to all of the three examples. *Firstly*—and fortunately—they are all hopefully low probability events that presumably happen only once in a rare while. *Secondly*, they are devastating and can completely destroy everything we worked so hard for—our family, our mental and physical health, our financial security, our careers, etc. Next, we can be impacted by such events even if we are several degrees removed from the trigger point. We may have the natural instincts to survive such calamities, but an ounce of prior-planning can give us a solid advantage while facing the ordeal and help us navigate out of the mess, to safe grounds.

Myriad things happen to us when we go through a crisis. We would get anxiety attacks—not knowing how long or how deep the crisis would be. Internal and external pressures would mount. A potpourri of emotions would occur—right from fear, anger and helplessness to downright shame, defeat and guilt. We may even have to go through a job change and be transplanted to an unknown and alien environment. Even if we held on to our jobs, our roles in our organizations can get marginalized. Yet others may be so traumatized that they will be in a 'reactive' mode, swept away by the tide, powerless to do anything about it. Note that:

a. Disaster-planning can be a part of our overall career planning strategy. Some of the ingredients used in disaster-planning like risk management and planning for contingencies, are also used in our career master plan.
b. Some of the habits that go into effectively dealing with disasters—such as anticipation, accepting that not everything can be anticipated, ice-cold nerves, alertness, sharp observation powers and instincts and carrying forward the lessons from a disaster—are good traits to have even under normal circumstances.

We will see that we need a large dose of this soft skill called *resilience—the* 'never say die' attitude—to tide over any calamity and to thrive in the post-disaster world.

From *The Ace of Soft Skills*, by Gopalaswamy Ramesh and Mahadevan Ramesh.

Exercise 1

Answer the following in one or two sentences:

i. What is the central idea of the above passage?

____

____

____

ii. What do you understand by the phrase 'programme manager got transferred to the Antarctica office.'

____

____

____

iii. What is the importance of resilience in the corporate world?

____

____

____

Dictionary Work

Find out the meanings of the following words and write them in the space provided below. Work in pairs:

- Trumped over: ______________________________
- Dog-eat-dog world: __________________________
- Fiasco: ____________________________________
- Trigger point: _______________________________
- Potpourri: __________________________________

Word Power

Note how the writer makes use of expressions such as 'sailing through our careers' and 'rough sea'. These are called analogies. An analogy is a comparison.

Could you think of more such expressions related to nature, and which signify difficult or uncomfortable situations in life and/or careers?

(Hint: Some examples can be found in the same paragraphs).

___

___

Now read the remaining part of the extract.

When Things Go Way Wrong ... Show Your Resilience

In good times, everyone will look like a winner—as long as you don't mess things up. But it takes a crisis to differentiate the strong, the poised and the resourceful ones from the rest of the flock. The fittest do not merely survive the ordeal and rise from the ashes like the mythological Phoenix, but also go on to become even more successful. Thus, resilience and how you handle crisis situations can really be a major differentiator as you progress further in your career.

Anticipate—Be prepared!

We cannot lightning-proof our lives. But we can do a thing or two by way of preparation, just in case a crisis descends down on us. Let us see how.

Anticipate what could go wrong: Being prepared is winning half the battle. Your first step should be to anticipate what things could go wrong and what kind of disasters or risks can strike you or your project. You can enumerate the possible disasters in two levels—first the category of disaster and the next the specific instances of possible disasters within that category.

Develop early warning systems to understand symptoms of potential disasters: A lot of disasters brew and slow-cook for some time before they erupt. The mango-drink fiasco probably developed over many months and we could have picked up the warning signals ahead of time if we were perceptive and kept our eyes and ears open to the environment. Advance warning is crucial to taking any kind of counter measure.

Look for troubling signs: Such signs would include an uncharacteristically frowning or introspective manager, too many closed door meetings, an unusually busy admin and of course, a yelling and screaming client who is threatening to pull out—just about any unusual activity. Keep checking on the health of your project in particular, through various sources. Read all e-mails carefully to see if there is anything between the lines. Check with other companies in your industry to see if there is a major systemic problem developing across the industry. Talk to outsiders and ask them for their insights. Are there unusually large numbers of people confined to the bench? Has the recruitment of new employees stopped? Are there any major contracts cancelled or scaled down? Have there been any shake-ups in the organization? Are there reports of any important strategic or tactical shifts in your company? Is there any hint of major belt-tightening?

Make sure that all the early warning signs add up. Quite often, we are not good at interpreting what we see in our radar screens and many times, early troubles may not be indicative of future bad trends. Sometimes a single piece of bad news can produce a knee-jerk reaction to jump into unnecessary alternative plans. That single piece could be an aberration that is unlikely to be indicative of any trend. The main point in developing these early warning signals is that the signals should show some *consistent* pattern.

Develop contingency and mitigation plans of how to react in a disaster, should the disaster materialize: Businesses manage their risks by coming up with alternative plans to complement their original plans, just in case the unexpected happens. So, whether you work in the administration or on the factory floor or in a BPO project, you will be required to operate out of a 'Plan B' in times of crisis. Discuss with your manager about your particular contingency plans, well in advance.

Determine the risks in your own job and see if you can devise back-up plans at the personal level. For example, if you are a software developer in an off-shoring project, what are the consequences if you cannot complete a critical module by a given deadline? Can you then re-negotiate the deadline? Can you deliver just a subset of the deliverables on the said deadline? Should you ask for more resources?

Contingency plans are very, very important. Sometimes they incorporate as much ingenuity as the original plan. The good ones are not only pragmatic, but also have the essentials of the initial plan and thus the impact of deviating from the main plan is minimized. Enough thought should also go into the disaster recovery part of any contingency plan, so that we are still on track to achieve most of our broad strategic goals we have set for ourselves.

Contingency plans apply not only to the project you are doing, but also to your own career and personal life. You have to ask yourself questions such as 'Will I have adequate cash flow to maintain my standard of living in case something drastic happens? For how long?' and so on. Of course, we caution you against dwelling on the negatives or spending too much time and effort on planning for contingencies.

One of the main ways of anticipating what could go wrong is to *stay connected*. Liaison with colleagues from your group as well as from other functions, your external business contacts and just about anyone who can add to your knowledge of the big picture. There is no better source of information than the human tongue. Of course, you should not spend half your workday chitchatting or rabble-rousing. But don't exist in a clamshell either, completely isolating yourself from everything else.

Also, you should know when to ring the alarm bells and embark on back-up plans. A moment too late and you will find yourself in a bigger mess. On the other hand, you don't want to use contingency plans in non-emergency situations. Don't break that piggy-bank yet, just because you are running a rupee too short!

Culture

The Phoenix is a mythical, sacred firebird found in the ancient mythologies of the Greeks and the Arabs. The Phoenix's ability to be reborn from its own ashes implies that it's immortal.

To rise like the Phoenix from the ashes suggests resilience.

Exercise 1

Answer the following questions.

i. What are the possible troubling signs at work?

____

____

____

ii. What does the writer mean by 'staying connected?'

____

____

____

iii. What contingency plan should one be prepared with?

____

____

____

Exercise 2

Make sentences with the words given:

i. anticipating:

____

ii. deadline:

____

iii. scaled down:

____

iv. liaison:

____

v. clamshell:

____

vi. rabble-rousing:

____

PRONUNCIATION

Numbers

Practise the pronunciation of the following words:

Nine thirty	One o' clock
Eight forty five	Three pm
Seven twenty	Five past nine
Eleven o'clock	Twenty minutes to eleven
Twelve am	Half past six

Facilities and Services at the Hotel

7

Situation
- Do you have an airport pick-up facility?
- Enquiring about the business centre

Grammar Bin
- Prepositions
- Prepositions in idioms

Speaking
- At the breakfast buffet

Real-life Reads
- Menus

Vocabulary
- What's cooking?

Workplace Skills
- At the hotel florist
- At the hotel coffee shop
- Expressing agreement

Pronunciation Practice
- Objects in a hotel room

SITUATION

Do You Have an Airport Pick-up Facility?

Sometimes, you might need to coordinate airport pick-ups and drops from the front desk of your hotel.

Discussion

What are those factors necessary to consider while picking up a guest from the airport? Discuss with your class. Now, read and practise the following conversation about a guest who needs an airport pick-up:

Employee: Hotel Sheraton. Thank you for calling. How may I help you?
Guest: Hi. My name is David Carrington. I have a reservation with you from 12 to 15 May.
Employee: Let me check that, sir. How do you spell your last name?
Guest: It is C-A-R-R-I-N-G-T-O-N.
Employee: Yes, sir. Your booking is confirmed. How may I assist you?
Guest: Well, I'm arriving on 12th May by 3 am IST, and was wondering if the hotel can arrange for a pick-up.
Employee: Certainly, sir. May I have your flight details, please?
Guest: It is CX 2359 from Hong Kong. Departure at 11.30 pm, arrival in MAA, that is, Chennai, at 3 am.
Employee: Very well, sir. We can certainly provide the facility at a charge. Our hotel car will be waiting for you at the main exit. The driver will be holding a placard with your name on it.
Guest: Perfect! And how far is the hotel from the airport?
Employee: It's nearly 30 minutes, sir. May we confirm the airport pick-up for you for your arrival by CX 2359 on 12th May 2012?
Guest: Yes, please make the arrangements for the pick-up. Thank you.
Employee: You're welcome. Have a safe and enjoyable journey, Mr Carrington.

Exercise 1

MAA is the airport code for Chennai. Can you match the following cities with their airport codes?

SL. NO.	AIRPORT CODE	SL. NO.	CITY
i.	AMS	a.	Bangkok
ii.	TXL	b.	Rio de Janeiro
iii.	BKK	c.	Amsterdam
iv.	FCO	d.	London
v.	GIG	e.	Rome
vi.	LHR	f.	Berlin
vii.	FRA	g.	Chicago
viii.	ORD	h.	Frankfurt

Enquiring About the Business Centre

Discussion

What facilities should a hotel business centre provide? What are the services most frequently requested by your clients?

Now read and practise the following conversation about a guest enquiring about the hotel's business centre:

Guest: Hi. I need some information about the business centre.
Employee: Certainly, sir. How can I help you?
Guest: Can you tell me about secretarial services available at the hotel?
Employee: Well, we have a fully equipped business centre, with facilities including secretarial services, computer services with Internet access, e-mail, faxes and so on. Our secretarial services include translation services as well. We also have video conferencing and Skype facilities.
Guest: That sounds great. I will need some translations done, particularly in French and Chinese.
Employee: That can be arranged easily, sir. Please let us know all your translation requirements 24 hours in advance and we can make the necessary arrangements to get the job done.
Guest: Good. I think that's all. And how much do you charge for all this?
Employee: Here's the price list; it contains the rates for individual services. The charges mentioned are exclusive of 12.5 per cent taxes.
Guest: Thank you.
Employee: You are welcome, sir. Please feel free to call us at our extension no. 503 and we shall be delighted to be of service. Have a nice day.

Essential Vocabulary: Business Centre

- **Video conferencing:** Conducting a conference between two or more participants at different sites by using computer networks to transmit audio and video data.
- **Skype:** A facility that enables users to make voice and video calls and chat over the Internet.
- **Secretarial services:** A group of people who provide services for clients, including reading and answering company e-mails, typing, organizing video conferencing, etc.

Exercise 1

Write the names of at least five secretarial services that your business centre provides. Explain them in a line each.

____

____

____

____

____

____

GRAMMAR BIN

Prepositions

A preposition expresses a relationship of meaning between two parts of a sentence. In the above conversation, for example, we have the sentence: 'And how much do you charge *for* all this?' Prepositions tell us how two parts of a sentence are related. We also use prepositions when we talk about somebody or something. Go through the following table to know more about prepositions and their functions:

Table 7.1 Prepositions and Their Uses

PREPOSITIONS	USES
At	To talk about a place as a point rather than area; also about an event where there is a group of people. *Example:* We arrived at the airport *at* 4 am.
On	To talk about a position touching a flat surface. *Example:* The menu is *on* the table.
In	To suggest a position within a larger area or space. *Example:* She is *in* the pool at the moment.
Across	To suggest a position on the other side of something, for example, a bridge, road, border, river, mountain, table, etc. *Example:* There is a famous hotel *across* the river.
Along	To talk about following a line of some kind. *Example:* He walked *along* the footpath till they came to the bridge.
Over	To talk about something at a higher level than another. *Example:* There was a big sign *over* the door saying, 'Beware of the dog.'
Through	*Through* discusses movement from one side or end of a space to the other. *Example:* He walked *through* the lobby to get to the gift shop.
Below/under	To suggest the opposite of over/above. *Example:* The cat is hiding *under* the table.
Between/among	*Between* suggests two or more people or things that we see as individuals or separate; we use among when we see the people or things as part of a group or mass. *Example: Between* you and me, I have never liked this place. Divide the money *among* all the friends.
By	We use *by* to suggest that one person or thing is at the side of another. *Example:* Steve sat *by* her as they waited for the bus.
Until	To suggest that something will continue up to a particular time. *Example:* The restaurant will remain open *until* 2.30.
About	*About* means 'concerning' or 'related to' something. *Example:* We didn't know *about* this hotel till someone told us about it.
With	It suggests how something is done using something. *Example:* Cut the vegetables *with* a sharp knife.

Exercise 1

Identify and correct the prepositions in the following sentences:

i. The key is below the carpet.
ii. The thieves broke the window and climbed in it.
iii. His head was under the level of the reception counter.
iv. She walked over the room to pick up the telephone.
v. They drove under the thick mist.
vi. Mary pointed at a place in the map and asked her mother about it.
vii. The Regent is on the next corner.

Prepositions in Idioms

Go through the following idioms and their meanings and note the use of prepositions in them.

i. **Over the moon:** To be very excited and happy.
   She was completely over the moon once she got the results.
ii. **Over the top:** To an excessive degree.
   The speaker went completely over the top during the course of the speech.
iii. **Under the weather:** To be unwell.
   Mary is rather under the weather and is on leave today.
iv. **Pull the wool over someone's eyes:** To deceive someone.
   It was clear that the salesman was pulling the wool over the customer's eyes.
v. **Over the hill:** To age.
   The actor is over the hill and should now make way for someone younger.
vi. **Behind the scenes:** Done, maintained, or held out of public view or in secret.
   The investigative reporter is doing a behind the scenes story of this incident.
vii. **From scratch:** From the beginning.
   Now that the dish is burnt we have to start it again from scratch.
viii. **Out of character:** Acting or behaving in an unusual manner.
   His sudden display of temper is completely out of character.
x. **Up in the air:** Uncertain.
   I am not sure about the new developments; the entire deal is up in the air.

Exercise 1

Fill in the blanks with the idioms given above:

i. The dish was burnt badly; the chef had to redo it ____________________.
ii. His anger was unjustified; he was completely ____________________.
iii. Redecorate the room; it's ____________________.
iv. The musician is feeling a little ____________________; and therefore would not be playing tonight.
v. We are not sure if the concert will be held tonight or not; it's all ____________________.

SPEAKING

At the Breakfast Buffet

Read the following conversation aloud with your partner:

Guest: These French toasts smell wonderful.
Employee: Thank you, Sir. Do try the waffles with sweet sauce as well.
Guest: They sure look good. I hope they taste good too. Don't they look slightly undercooked?
Employee: Not at all. I'll get some to your table. They are done just right. Would you like me to get some well-done ones to your table? We could also add some chocolate sauce if you wish.
Guest: No thanks. I've got to watch my calories.
Employee: And how about some fruit, sir?
Guest: That would be great. Thank you.
Employee: Would you like to have your coffee now or later?
Guest: Now, please. I would prefer black, without sugar.
Employee: Certainly, sir.

Discussion
Discuss with your class:

- If you worked in a hotel, what would usually be served for breakfast there?
- What do people in your country have for breakfast when they're at home?

Exercise 1
Take turns to play the role of a guest and a staff member of a hotel with your partner. The guest has some queries about the dinner buffet. Respond to her/him. You may cover the following:

- Details of the complimentary mocktail
- Soup of the day
- Post-buffet coffee
- Billing

REAL-LIFE READS

Menus

Three of your hotel guests have indicated the number of orders, time and preferences for breakfast. Read the menus given below and answer the questions that follow:

Menu 1

BREAKFAST

Date	Room No.	Name	No. of Persons	To be served at
12 October 2011	342	Mr Dhananjayan R	2	9.00 am
13 October 2011			2	8.00 am

AMERICAN BREAKFAST Orders

₹600

Juice	Orange	Pineapple	Grapes
Eggs	Fried	Scrambled	Boiled
Bread	With ham/butter/cheese/marmalade/jam		
Beverage	Tea/coffee/hot chocolate/milk		

CONTINENTAL BREAKFAST Orders

₹400

Juice	Orange	Pineapple	Grapes
Bread	With ham/butter/cheese/marmalade/jam		
Beverage	Tea/coffee/chocolate/milk		

Menu 2

BREAKFAST

Date	Room No.	Name	No. of Persons	To be served at
12 October 2011	403	Mr Dilip Kumar Sharma	1	7.30 am
13 October 2011			3	9.30 am
14 October 2011			3	8.30 am

AMERICAN BREAKFAST Orders

₹600

Juice	Orange	Pineapple	Grapes
Eggs	Fried	Scrambled	Boiled
Bread	With ham/butter/cheese/marmalade/jam		
Beverage	Tea/coffee/hot chocolate/milk		

CONTINENTAL BREAKFAST Orders

₹400

Juice	Orange	Pineapple	Grapes
Bread	With ham/butter/cheese/marmalade/jam		
Beverage	Tea/coffee/chocolate/milk		

Menu 3

BREAKFAST

Date	Room No.	Name	No. of Persons	To be served at
12 October 2011	1152	Mr Roger Nunan	2	8.00 am
13 October 2011			2	8.00 am

AMERICAN BREAKFAST Orders

₹600

Juice	Orange	Pineapple	Grapes
Eggs	Fried	Scrambled	Boiled
Bread	With ham/butter/cheese/marmalade/jam		
Beverage	Tea/coffee/hot chocolate/milk		

CONTINENTAL BREAKFAST Orders

₹400

Juice	Orange	Pineapple	Grapes
Bread	With ham/butter/cheese/marmalade/jam		
Beverage	Tea/coffee/chocolate/milk		

Exercise 1

Based on the information given above, answer the questions that follow:

i. When does Mr Dhananjayan want his breakfast on 12 October?

____

ii. Who is staying in Room no. 1152?

____

iii. How many persons are staying in 403?

____

iv. How many days will Mr Dilip Kumar stay in the hotel?

____

v. When does Mr Roger Nunan want his breakfast?

____

vi. How does Mr Dhananjayan prefer his eggs?

____

vii. Which style of breakfast does Mr Nunan prefer?

____

Culture Corner

Here are some Western holidays and celebrations. Can you match the days, dates and special meals for that particular day with each other?

DAYS	DATES	SPECIAL MEALS
Independence Day	USA: fourth Thursday in November/Canada: second Monday in October	Turkey, cranberry sauce, sweet potato casserole, pumpkin pie, peas, corn
Christmas	4 July	Cakes, pies, ham, turkey, Christmas stolen, eggnog, wine
Thanksgiving Day	25 December	Hot dogs, roasted marshmallows, hamburgers, pickles, potato chips, pork and beans, pie, ice cream

VOCABULARY

What's Cooking?

Here are some terms related to cooking and baking. Use them in sentences of your own:

Baking: ____________________

Basted: ____________________

Dice: ____________________

Deep fry: ____________________

Defrost: ____________________

Fillet: ____________________

Garnish: ____________________

Season: ____________________

Poaching: ____________________

Mash: ____________________

Simmer: ____________________

Mince: ____________________

Roast: ____________________

Stew: ____________________

Steam: ____________________

Toast: ______________________________

Broil (British/Indian English = Grill): ______________________________

Frozen: ______________________________

Deep frost: ______________________________

Flambé (Food covered with alcohol, especially brandy and allowed to burn for a short while. Must have flames when served at the table or 'flamed' on the trolley when prepared next to the table.):

____

Grate: ______________________________

WORKPLACE SKILLS

At the Hotel Florist

Practise the following conversation with a partner:

Saleswoman: Good morning. 'The Fragrance.' May I help you?
Derek: Hi, My name is Derek Nevelson. I'd like to order some flowers and have them delivered to my client's house.
Salesperson: All right, Mr Nevelson. What kind of flowers do you have in mind?
Derek: Well, you see, it's their first wedding anniversary and I was thinking about some red roses. What would you say to that?
Salesperson: Red roses seem just fine. As a matter of fact, they are the appropriate flowers for most occasions. How many would you like to send?
Derek: May be a dozen, with long stems.
Salesperson: That would cost you ₹1000, inclusive of taxes.
Derek: That's okay. I'll take those.
Salesperson: Could you please give me the name and the complete address of the person to whom you would like us to deliver the flowers?
Derek: Sure. It's to be sent to Mr and Mrs Sen at 24, Safdarjung Enclave, flat number 25.
Salesperson: All right. What would you like to put on the card?
Derek: Umm, how about 'With best wishes and love?'
Salesperson: Sounds good, simple and precise. When would you like us to deliver them to Mr Sen?
Derek: This 24 September, between nine and ten in the morning.
Salesperson: Certainly, Mr Nevelson. Just one last question, how would you like to make the payment, please?
Derek: You can put it on my credit card. Here you are.
Salesperson: Thank you Mr Nevelson. May we request your signature on the charge slip? Thank you very much. We will deliver a dozen red roses to Mr and Mrs Sen on 24th September between 9 am and 10 am. Have a nice day.

At the Hotel Coffee Shop

Exercise 1

Complete the following dialogue at the coffee shop by placing these jumbled responses in the correct order:

One large, strong, black blend of Brazilian and Columbian

Thank you

Yeah. I'd like to have a large sub, please.

Um, I don't really think so. But I'd appreciate some coffee

No, thanks

Server: May I take your order, please?

Guest: ____

Server: Would you like to have anything else to go with it?

Guest: ____

Server: Certainly, would you like some soup to go with your order?

Guest: ____

Server: How would you like your coffee?

Guest: ____

Server: Right away.

Guest: ____

Expressing Agreement

Exercise 1

Make sentences with the following expressions indicating agreement. Then, practise speaking with your partner using the following expressions:

1. **Undoubtedly:** __________________________________
2. **Sure:** __________________________________
3. **I agree (with you):** __________________________________
4. **I quite agree with you:** __________________________________
5. **Exactly:** __________________________________
6. **Quite right:** __________________________________
7. **Quite true:** __________________________________

8. **Absolutely:** ____________________
9. **Certainly:** ____________________
10. **Positively:** ____________________

PRONUNCIATION PRACTICE

Objects in a Hotel Room

Read out the list of objects in a hotel room, as given below:

- CD Player
- Coat Hangers
- Radio Alarm
- Writing desk
- Remote control
- Flowers
- Laundry bag
- Personal safe
- Duvet
- Central light switch
- Air-conditioning
- Suitcase stand

8

PLACES AROUND THE HOTEL

In This Unit

Situation
- Give directions
- Identify locations and streets

Reading Comprehension
- Touring Malaysia

Vocabulary
- Word formation using suffixes
- Common spelling rules

Grammar
- Expressing approximation
- Subject verb agreement

Speaking
- Everyday expressions

Pronunciation Practice
- Negative contractions

Language Focus
- Fun with language

SITUATION

Giving Directions

A guest needs directions to a famous shopping mall and other landmarks of the city. Read and practise the following conversation:

Guest: Hi, we're planning to go to the Pizzeria. Could you tell us how to get there?
Receptionist: Certainly, sir. You can go straight and take the left, you'll be on SP Road. You'll find Crescent, a big shopping mall. You need to walk down a couple of blocks, and you'll find the Pizzeria.
Guest: Thanks. And how do we go to the City Museum from there?
Receptionist: You can take a cab till MG Road. The museum is right across the street.
Guest: And how far is MG Road from SP Road?
Receptionist: It's a nearly 30-minute drive. Here, let me give you the brochure. It has all the landmarks of our city.
Guest: Great. It even has a map. Thank you so much.
Receptionist: You're welcome, sir. Have a nice day.

Essential Vocabulary
Make sentences with the words given below:

- Left
- Right
- Around
- Straight
- Next
- Beside
- Opposite
- Across

Identify Locations and Streets

A guest needs help with locations and streets. Read and practise the following conversation:

Guest: Hi, could you tell me how to get to the Big Market?
Receptionist: Sure, madam. You can go straight and take the second left from there; you'll come across Quality Theatre. Big Market is right opposite Quality.
Guest: Thank you. And is there any book shop around?
Receptionist: There is, madam. We have Ovid's next to Big Market; it is one of the biggest bookshops in Asia.

Guest: That's nice. And what exactly is the street called?
Receptionist: It is AR Road, madam. There's a big, green signboard down this street with its name. You won't miss it.
Guest: Alright; thank you so much.
Receptionist: You're welcome, madam.

You might find the following websites useful for improving your vocabulary:

- *http://www.englisch-hilfen.de/en/words/asking_the_way_vocabulary.htm*
- *www.ego4u.com/en/cram-up/vocabulary/directions*
- *www.free-english-study.com/speaking/giving-direction.html*

Web Sites

READING COMPREHENSION

Touring Malaysia

Pre-reading Activity
Make a presentation on any site of historical importance in your country. You can discuss the following points:

- The story behind who made it, and why
- What makes it relevant today
- What are its main attractions

Reading
Read the following passage on major events in Malaysia and answer the questions that follow:

The Enchanting History of Malaysia

Located on the famous Straits of Malacca, a few hundred kilometers away from Kuala Lumpur, Malacca is a place with a glorious past. However, not much was known about the state until the 15th century as there were no proper records prior to this period. According to the historical records, it was founded by an exiled Hindu prince, Parameswara, from Palembang in Sumatra in 1402. Melaka then grew slowly but steadily to become a major trading centre and port for ships from the four corners of the world. Among them were ships of Indian–Muslim traders from India whose wealth attracted Parameswara. Soon, he too embraced Islam and came to be known as Megat Iskandar Shah. Hence began the Melaka Sultanate.

In 1409, Admiral Cheng Ho, an envoy of the Ming Emperor, helped forge links between the state and the Middle Kingdom. This was the beginning of a long relationship between Melaka and

China. The descendants of Chinese settlers from this period were products of a unique fusion of traditional Chinese origins and Malay upbringing.

The Melaka Sultanate flourished to become the emporium of the East and its prosperity soon made it a target for the growing Portuguese empire. In 1509, a Portuguese galleon headed by De Sequeira landed at Melaka. Impressed by the state's beauty and wealth, he tried to overthrow the Malay kingdom but was thwarted by Sultan Mahmud, the leader then. The Sultanate reigned until a Portuguese army attack led by Alfonso De Albuquerque in 1511.

The Portuguese continued to rule Melaka against all odds until they were ousted by the ambitious and more powerful Dutch in 1641. The 19th century began a period of British rule until the country's independence in 1957. Despite the recent appearances of modern buildings and hotels on the periphery of the old town, Melaka still remains an interesting historical site. All cultural and architectural relics of the respective colonial eras can still be seen today.

(*Source*: http://www.marimari.com/content/malaysia/events_festivals/main.html)

Exercise 1

Tell a guest about a strategically located landmark in your city. Explain the importance of the place and give directions. Exchange roles.

Exercise 2

Answer the following questions:

i. Describe the relationship between China and Malaysia.

____

____

ii. How did the Melaka Sultanate begin?

____

____

iii. Why does the writer call Melaka an interesting historical site?

____

____

Exercise 3

Fill in the blanks using the words given in the box below:

Exile	Thwarted	Strategically
Fusion	Slowly	

i. The museum is ______________ located between the forts.

ii. The train ______________ arrived at platform no. 6.

iii. The president was forced to live in ______________.
iv. All his efforts to destabilize the firm have been ______________ by the team.
v. The cuisine is a ______________ of the East and the West.

VOCABULARY

Word Formation Using Suffixes

A suffix is a letter or a group of letters added to the end of a word to make another word. The suffix '-ship', when added to a word gives the sense of domain or status.

Thus, FRIEND+SHIP = FRIENDSHIP and DICTATOR+SHIP = DICTATORSHIP.

Similarly, the suffix '-ocracy' gives us words like 'aristocracy' and 'democracy'.

Here is a list of suffixes, which can help you in understanding difficult words.

Table 8.1 Words Formed Using Suffixes

SUFFIX	MEANING	EXAMPLES
-ment	A state, to fulfil something	Disillusionment, contentment, excitement, encouragement
-er	For a person who does an activity	Cleaner, driver, smoker
-ist	For a person who has certain beliefs, ideologies and politics. Also, for their professions	Idealist, leftist, dentist
-ity, ly	A state or feeling; Having the characteristics of	Hostility, ability, friendly, girly, costly, sensitively, happily
-ize	To make/do something	Sensitize, customize, revolutionize
-hood	A state of being something	Childhood, girlhood, selfhood
-ship, -ish	A state of being something	Relationship, hardship, slavish, foolish, snobbish
-ful	A state of being something	Forgetful, forceful
-less	Without	Clueless, sugarless, bottomless

Exercise 1

Give a one word substitute for each of the following sentences, using the words given in the above list:

i. She has no idea about what is going on. ______________
ii. He has the quality of treating people equally or in a way that is reasonable. ______________
iii. Children love the holiday season and feel a great deal of happiness and enthusiasm as it approaches. ______________
iv. The restaurant refuses to accept the entry of people not dressed formally and is fussy about appearances. ______________
v. She is often forgetting things. ______________

Exercise 2

Given below is a list of suffixes. Make at least three words with each.

i. -ful

____

____

____

ii. -like

____

____

____

iii. -ing

____

____

____

iv. -ment

____

____

____

v. -ly

____

____

____

Common Spelling Rules

A common mistake while spelling is in the use of words like 'receive' and 'achieve', where users are often unsure about the order of the vowels *e* and *i*. The well-known rhyme goes, '*i* before *e*, except after *c*'. But the complete rule is: When the vowel sound is *i*, represent the sound by spelling *ie*; but after *c*, it is spelt as *ei*.

Here are some examples:

Table 8.2 Spelling Rules

ie Words	Words with *ei* after *c*
Achieve	Deceive
Fiend	Conceive
Grief	Receive
Siege	Perceive
Fief	Conceit

A simple rule is that the words which have the *ei* pattern in their verb forms, take the suffix *–tion* in their noun forms.

Example: *conception, reception, deception,* and *perception.*

Exceptions with *ei* representing the sound *i* when it does not come after *c* are: *protein, heinous, counterfeit, caffeine, seize.* Also, there are a number of words with *ei* which may or may not have the sound *i,* as in *heifer, weight, height, neither, heir, deity, weird, reign, neighbour.* Similarly, in the spelling *ie,* there are words which do not have the sound *i* such as: *science, financier, conscience, sufficient, friend.*

In spite of the above discussion, you must know that there are no hard and fast rules of spelling in the English language, and practising regularly is the best means to master this skill.

Remember!

The adjectives dependent *and* independent *are spelt with –ent at the end.*
Example: *The way you perform in your exams is* dependent *on a number of factors.*
The word dependant*, on the other hand, is a noun which refers to a person who depends on someone else financially.*
Example: *The institute provides free hospitality for employees and their* dependants.

Exercise 1

Fill in the blanks with appropriate vowels. Check your answers in a dictionary:

i. Defin_te
ii. Hypocr_sy
iii. Fr_volous
iv. Rep_tition
v. Permiss_ble
vi. Adapt_ble
vii. Feas_ble
viii. Predict_ble
ix. Sal_ _ble
x. Convert_ble

GRAMMAR

Expressing Approximation

Often we come across phrases such as 'about $50 per month' or 'nearly ₹200,000'. What is meant here is that the cost of something is not exactly $50; it can range, for example, between $45 and $55. Consider the sentence, 'There are around 500 theatres in Delhi and approximately 20 per cent are being renovated.' In this sentence, again, we are not talking about the exact number of theatres in Delhi; also we are not sure about the accurate number of theatres that are under renovation.

Some words that express approximation are:

Approximately	Almost	Give or take	Or thereabouts
About	Nearly	More or less	Somewhere in the region of
Around	Roughly	Or so	

Can you think of more examples? Write them down in the space given.

Exercise 1

Huntingdon Pvt Ltd is a leading name in the production of laser printers. Given below is an excerpt from the company profile. Rewrite the information, using expressions of approximation.

Example: Huntingdon Pvt Ltd spends *somewhere in the region* of $3689 annually on print publicity.

Percentage of sales in Asia	34.78
Amount spent on charity	$1billion
Funds under management	$12,466 billion
Number of major research and development centres worldwide	127
Number of strategic business centres	1,244
Number of non-American employees	8,673

Exercise 2

Fill in the blanks using the appropriate phrases given in the box below:

Beat on	Broke up with	Bust up
Doss down	Gone through	Punch out
Gets off	Break away	Rub out
Have a bite		

i. Everyone _______ _______ work on Sunday.
ii. After she _______ _______ _______ Anthony, Sally has been feeling low.
iii. You look tired, go and _______ _______.
iv. I've already _______ _______ my paycheck for the week, and now I'm completely broke.
v. He _______ _______ Clark so hard that he nearly fell down.
vi. An eminent scientist has been mysteriously _______ _______.

Subject Verb Agreement

Look at the following sentences:

- All these factors have resulted in accelerating an abiding interest in reading.
- Patrons agree that the Web has made libraries easier to use.

Both the above sentences have plural subjects: *factors* and *patrons*. Therefore, we use plural verbs with them, such as *have* and *agree*, respectively.

Agreement of the subject and verb refers to the fact that the verb changes depending on the type of noun used.

Subject

As you know, the subject in a sentence is an agent or a doer. For example, in the sentence, 'The chef is preparing steak today.' the *chef* is the doer of the action, and *is,* the singular verb.

In the sentence, 'The waiters are working long hours.' the noun *waiters* is the subject and *are*, the plural verb.

Verbs

Most verbs tell what someone does: give, take, eat, sleep, go, come, do, think, etc.

Be and *have*: These two verbs have multiple forms.

Example: am, being, is, are, was, were, have, has, had, having.

But there is another category of verbs as well. These are known as auxiliaries or helping verbs: will, would, shall, should, may, might, can, could and must.

The auxiliary verb *do* takes the following forms: do, does, did, doing, done.

The verb *let* is used for first and second person imperatives.

Example: *Let* us walk fast.
Let the instruments get sterilized.
Let the matron decide the duties.

Exercise 1

Identify the subject and the verbs in the following sentences:

i. We attended a talk by an ace corporate trainer.
Subject: ____________________
Verb: ____________________

ii. I know I am going to be late today.
Subject: ____________________
Verb: ____________________

iii. They were asked to demonstrate receiving international visitors.
Subject: ____________________
Verb: ____________________

iv. There is a shortage of trained chefs in our hotels.
Subject: ____________________
Verb: ____________________

v. The waiters are working in the dining hall.
Subject: ____________________
Verb: ____________________

vi. LEDs are very expensive.
Subject: ____________________
Verb: ____________________

vii. The fax machine is currently out of order.
Subject: ____________________
Verb: ____________________

viii. There are three conference halls in this hotel.
Subject: ____________________
Verb: ____________________

SPEAKING

Everyday Expressions

Practise speaking with your partner using the following expressions:

1.	For getting someone's attention	Excuse me Hello Yes?
2.	Confirmation	Yes Sure I agree Exactly

PRONUNCIATION PRACTICE

Negative Contractions

Practise saying the negative contractions given in the list below.

aren't	isn't
weren't	wasn't
don't	doesn't
didn't	haven't
hasn't	hadn't

LANGUAGE FOCUS

Fun with Language

What are the familiar sights and sounds you find when you return to your hometown after a journey? Use the following table to name some.

Natural landmarks	Rivers, lakes, hills mountains	
Historical monuments	Forts, palaces	
Tourist spots	Beaches, backwaters	The sound of waves, people sunbathing
Manmade buildings/ places/streets	Hotels, resorts, cinema theatres, gardens, railway station, famous streets, shopping areas, market places	
Religious places	Temples, churches, mosques, synagogues	
Sounds	Traffic, people, public announcements	

9

GETTING A DUPLICATE KEY

Situation
- Getting a duplicate key
- Apologizing for a mistake

Grammar Bin
- *Can* and *could*

Reading Comprehension
- Hotel lobbies

Language Focus
- Handling complaints and making suggestions

Workplace Skills
- Soft skills

Pronunciation Practice
- Hotel names and other words

Appreciating Literature
- *The Phantom Luncheon* by Saki

SITUATION

Getting a Duplicate Key for a Guest

Mr Sen has lost his key card and requests for a duplicate one at the Reception. Read and practise the following conversation:

Receptionist: Good evening, sir.
Guest: Hi, I have a little problem. You see, we went out for sightseeing and somewhere along the way, I lost the key card to our room. Could I have a duplicate, please?
Receptionist: Certainly, sir. May I have your room number please? It is 211, isn't it?
Guest: It is 211.
Receptionist: Thank you, Mr Sen. For your security, may we request you to sign this form and also show us a photo identity?
Guest: Of course. And here is my driving licence.
Receptionist: Thank you, Mr Sen. It will take just a few seconds for us to photocopy the licence and configure a new key card.
Guest: That's alright.
Receptionist: I'll call the housekeeping on your floor, sir. Someone will be there with a duplicate key.
(after a few minutes)
Receptionist: Mr Sen, here is your driving licence and a new key card for your room number 211. For your own safety and security, the previous key card has been deactivated and cannot be used to open any door.
Guest: Thank you so much.
Receptionist: You're welcome, sir.

Apologizing for a Mistake

Discussion
What are the different situations where you may have to apologize to a guest for some reason? Note a few down in the following space. Then, enact one such situation with your partner.

___

___

___

A receptionist apologizes for a malfunctioning room key. Read and practise the following conversation:

Receptionist: Good afternoon, sir.
Guest: Hi. Could you check my room key, please? It doesn't seem to work.
Receptionist: Certainly. Please can I have the key?
Guest: I think you didn't charge it enough. It was working alright until this morning.

Receptionist: That's right, sir. It needs to be re-activated.
Guest: I wish you were more responsible about such things. It does seem that your staff is quite careless about basic services.
Receptionist: I'm extremely sorry for the inconvenience, sir. I assure you this won't happen again. For your safety and security, we activate key cards for 72 hours from the time of check-in and subsequently re-activate it as a policy. I apologize for not having informed you of this. However, should you wish, we could activate it up to your date of departure.
Guest: Alright. Please ensure that it is activated till I checkout on the 5th.
Receptionist: Certainly, sir. It will take just a few seconds. Here it is. The key card for your room has been activated for use until you check out on 5 April.
Guest: Thank you.
Receptionist: You're welcome, sir. And I do apologize for the inconvenience caused.

Exercise 1
Based on the above conversations, complete the following sentences using the verbs *can*, *could* or *have*.

i. ____________ you got a duplicate key?
ii. ____________ you get me another key, please?
iii. ____________ the hotel got a gym?
iv. I ____________ a problem.
v. ____________ we use the sauna now?

GRAMMAR BIN

Can and *Could*

Can suggests the ability to do something. We use *could* to show that we are giving an opinion; or suggesting a possibility or a past possibility. *Could* is also used when we want to be particularly polite. Look at the following sentences:

- It *could* rain later.
- It *could* be that his flight got delayed.
- During the earthquake, the hotel *could* have caught fire.

Exercise 1
Fill in the blanks with *can/could*.

i. The map was destroyed before it ____________ be read by the enemy.
ii. The bird ____________ be recognized by the red specks on its feathers.
iii. Whether the disease is infectious ____________ be detected just by looking at the patient's tongue.
iv. The secretary ____________ translate in Spanish.
v. ____________ I use your car, please?

READING COMPREHENSION

Hotel Lobbies

Pre-reading Activity

Describe a hotel lobby. Make a presentation on its important features.

Reading

Now read the following passage on hotel lobbies:

Hotel Lobbies as Social Spaces

A lobby is the first place to attract attention the moment a guest steps into a hotel. Frequent travellers would have noticed that hotel lobbies have become more social. Hotels no longer limit themselves to providing free wi-fi to guests. As we become more interested in working in shared spaces, hotels are trying to become more like the coffee shops and other hangouts where we work. The trend can be observed across the spectrum, from lower-priced discount hotels to higher-end properties,like A-Loft (Starwood's lower-end designer label), Hyatt (both their restaurant-less Hyatt Palace, and extended-stay Hyatt House brands), Marriott Courtyards and Hilton's Home2 Suites extended stay brands. Hotels now want to remake the sterile and impersonal hotel lobby into a 'social hub' that is more living room than just a place to check in and grab a free newspaper and wait for a taxi.

Besides free broadband, these new lobbies feature several attractions to keep guests engaged, such as free happy hours, huge touchscreen TVs running information portal pages on information like the weather at their next destination and comfortable seating that looks more like your own living room, although one that has a lot more space and tables where you can place your laptop or food from the breakfast bar. Art lounges, fire places, bookshelves and even ping pong tables are fast-becoming a common sight around the lobbies.

The Hyatt House hotels have new seating which is inspired by the airlines. There are built-in charging plugs and a place to rest your laptop and other gadgets. For the past several years, Marriott Courtyards have been deploying what they call 'GoBoards' or interactive concierge touchscreen portals.

The A-Loft hotel brand is also experimenting in a few of their hotels a 'smart check in' feature. If you are a Starwood Preferred Guest programme member, you are sent an RFID keycard in the mail. On the day of a planned stay, a text message is sent to your mobile with a room number and you can go directly to your room, without having to stop at the front desk. The same technology is used at A-Lofts in Brooklyn and Harlem in New York City, Lexington, Massachusetts, Dallas, Jacksonville, Florida and London. The Oslo Comfort Xpress hotel has automated lobby kiosks that dispense RFID room cards.

(*Source:* http://www.readwriteweb.com/enterprise/2011/09/hotel-lobbies-become-more-soci.php)

Exercise 1

Answer the following questions.

i. What were hotel lobbies like in earlier times?

____

____

ii. Mention any three specific features of modern hotel lobbies.

____

____

____

____

iii. How is the Hyatt lobby comparable with airline seating arrangements?

____

____

Essential Vocabulary

- **Sterile:** (here) monotonous
- **Kiosk:** A pavilion like structure, open on all sides
- **Cues:** hints, ideas
- **Dispense:** (here) supply a product
- **Concierge:** An employee who either works in shifts within, or lives on the premises of an apartment building or a hotel; (here) a kind of marketing platform

Exercise 1

Match the following:

i.	A-Loft	a.	RFID keycard
ii.	Marriott Courtyards	b.	Automated lobby kiosks
iii.	The Oslo Comfort Xpress hotel	c.	Starwood's lower-end designer label
iv.	Starwood Preferred Guest programme member	d.	'GoBoards'

Exercise 2

Complete the following:

i. Of late, hotel lobbies have become more ____________.
ii. The hotels are becoming like ____________ where we hang out.
iii. A hotel is no longer just a place to check in and grab a free newspaper and wait for a ____________.
iv. The Hyatt Place has built-in charging plugs and a place to rest your laptop and ____________.

LANGUAGE FOCUS

Handling Complaints and Making Suggestions

Table 9.1 Expressions for Handling Complaints and Making Suggestions

EXPRESSIONS	SIGNIFICANCE
Please hold on	Request which suggests that the caller wait for a while since the person at the other end of the line is busy
Please	Request for something
I'm extremely sorry	Apologizing
I wonder if I could	Starting to make a request
Good bye	Taking leave of someone
Have a safe journey	Wishing somebody who is going on a journey

In the dialogues above, we have seen the way the receptionist answers the client's queries with courtesy and patience. It is important for an employee to present his/her hotel in the best light. For this, he should be able to handle complaints effectively, along with taking responsibility for a mistake and apologizing for the inconvenience caused to the patrons.

Example: *Your complaint is justified* and I shall look into the matter immediately.

I'm extremely sorry, but the hotel is full. *Would you like us to* suggest an alternative?

Exercise 1

Look at the following sentences and fill in the blanks with the appropriate phrases given in the box:

a. There seems to have been a mistake at our end.
b. We shall do our best to compensate you.
c. Kindly wait for a moment, we shall sort it out.
d. May I help you?
e. Perhaps you'd like to speak to Mr North about it.

i. I'm afraid, I do not handle this department ________________.
ii. You are right about the missing piece of luggage ________________.
iii. Hotel Eleanor ________________.
iv. We are so sorry about this confusion regarding your reservation ________________.
v. It appears that there is an error in your bill ________________.

Exercise 2

Strike out the phrases that you think sound impolite or unprofessional:

1.	Could you tell me your name please?	5.	May I help you?
2.	What can I do for you?	6.	No problem
3.	What do you want?	7.	How can I help you?
4.	That can be easily arranged for, sir	8.	This is not our fault

WORKPLACE SKILLS

Soft Skills

Pre-reading Activity

What are soft skills? Why do we need to develop soft skills at all? Discuss with your partner.

Reading

Now read the following extract and answer the questions below:

Are you ready for soft skills?

Modern corporations offer an exciting work environment that rewards merit and hard work over bureaucracy and job titles. Soft skills are a big part of this 'merit' and can indeed be a major differentiator between successful and not-so-successful employees in an organization. However, you should know that there is a long and exhaustive list of such soft skills, making it difficult to cultivate them in a hurry or to do it in an organic fashion. Rather, you have to take the trouble to master these skills in a methodical manner, with a lot of grit and effort. Despite the complexity of the process, workplaces expect their star employees to possess and deploy a wide array of soft skills.

We want you to understand that each soft skill has a role to play at work and even if two soft skills seem similar, there are subtle differences between them. Your success in developing soft skills is dictated by how well you can combine these different soft skills to suit your personal style, your environment and each specific situation you face.

Finally, we want to instill in you that burning desire to improve your soft skills and motivate you to go beyond a superficial window dressing. We believe this is the single most important ingredient we bring to the table—enabling you to change your attitude, improve your communication and fine-tune your etiquette. We want you to stir yourself from within and create in yourself a paradigm shift in the way you think, act and talk. We then want you to take the next step and actually embark on a personal mission to improve the level of your own soft skills.

How do you motivate yourself to go after a skill? How do you motivate yourself to get rid of bad habits and practices? By consciously telling yourself '*Yes, I can do it*'. It is like remembering the pot of gold at the end of the rainbow. It is by looking at all the role models you have in front of you. It can be achieved through listening to mentors and self-improvement experts enunciate the need for attitude adjustment. It is made possible by deep introspection and convincing yourself that the change in attitude is necessary and for the better.

If your question is, 'How do I move forward?', this is how we would like you to move ahead:

Take stock: A journey always starts with knowing where you are. And believe us, you already have something of each of these soft skills in you, waiting to be tapped, nurtured and developed. Rather than looking at the glass as half-full and grouching about the soft skills that (you think) you don't have, focus on those soft skills that you do possess and which are your strengths. Then you know where to start from. At the same time, don't be oblivious about your weaknesses. Not having a particular strength may not be as bad as not knowing your weaknesses! As far as soft skills are concerned, ignorance is *not* bliss. But *how do you know where you are today on any of your skills? How do you take stock?* This is indeed a difficult question. You have to examine yourself extremely objectively or get feedback from your well-wishers, mentors, managers and others to arrive at a baseline score for where you are on specific soft skills.

Build on your strengths: When you set out to build on your strengths you will find that there are certain sets of soft skills that are somewhat related to each other. For example, the communication vehicles are all related. Similarly, teamwork and diversity are related. For instance, if you are already working well with your Indian teammates but are not so effective in the English language, you can attempt to work with an international team with members from other cultures. This way, while contributing to the multi-cultural team with your team intelligence, you can also benefit from it by improving your English language skills.

Prioritize what you want you to improve: As we have said before in this book, if everything is important, nothing is important. You simply must not dilute your pri- orities and stretch yourself too thin. Focus on a few soft skills at a time and put a plan in place to improve those skills. You can also pluck a few low hanging fruits by honing the less-abstract skills like e-mail etiquette and phone etiquette, while working on the more abstract ones like the vision for the long term. Improving some skills may be as simple as getting rid of some annoying bad habits (like being habitually late for appointments). Again, prioritize and strategize how you plan to go about improving your soft skills set. Don't keep scores on how many soft skills you have conquered or how many more are left to go. Just do it!

Grab opportunities that come by: Soft skills cannot be improved by sitting at home and just brooding over improvement. Like cycling, it improves by practice. Use any formal learning resource, where available (short courses, books, lectures, etc.), to learn the soft skills effectively. Assiduously practise what you have learnt. In a business environment, there are ample opportunities that come your way. It is up to you to grab such opportunities with both hands and try to polish your skills. Better still, be on the lookout for opportunities, openings and special circumstances where you can step in and display your new personality. Developing a reputation takes time, but persistence pays off.

Don't be afraid to make mistakes: Mistakes are part of a learning experience. As someone said, 'A ship is safest in the harbour, but that is not what it was designed for.' So don't let the fear of failure come in the way of executing your self-improvement plan.

Set yourself targets: Just telling yourself 'I will improve my soft skills' is not sufficient. You need to set yourself targets. For example, if you are concentrating on your presentation skills, try to have numerical goals where possible—such as trying to improve your instructor rating from your current rating of, say, 7 out of 10 to 9 out of 10, by next year. Or you can have other measurable targets like trying to do 30 per cent more presentations this year than last year.

Don't try too many things at one time: Seeing the long list of soft skills can make you feel scared. It is possible that you may tell yourself 'Wow, I know I lack in time management and meeting management and I don't have a clear vision and I know I am considered a bore and I need to improve my use of humour. Let me embark on all these things from today.' Trying too many things at the same time will lead you nowhere. They may simply pull you in different directions and would in fact, be detrimental to your soft skills. As we said in the preceding paragraphs, do start from your positions of strength and build on those areas.

Don't be a perfectionist and try to get '100 per cent' in any one soft skill before going to the next: Soft skills are not like theorem-proving in geometry, where every step depends on the completion of the previous step. If you try to be a perfectionist in honing one skill to 'perfection' before going on to the next, you will get nowhere. You may never have the time to be perfect in every single soft skill outlined here— but you can do the next best thing. You can be reasonably perfect in several of them, very good in many others and competent in the rest of them—enough to stand out, overall.

Constantly review, revise and refine your strategy: Improving soft skills is a moving target. What is 'good soft skills' today may be completely inappropriate tomorrow; what is appropriate in one culture may be completely unacceptable in another. Hence, it is important to have your antennae up all the time.

There are no short cuts: Our approach is always *values-based*. We do not recommend any short cuts or unethical or uncouth methods to acquire soft skills or to be used in place of soft skills. We have left out shrewdness, cunning, Shylock- style vengefulness, avarice and so on from our discussions, even if some people may profit from such things in a business environment. A values-based approach should never be compromised on.

Be patient! And finally, we want you to realize that changing one's habits, acquiring a soft skill or exercising a high level of control over one's work life can be quite an arduous process, consuming a lot of time and effort. This is not one of those processes that offer instant gratification. You should be aware that success comes slowly over time and one has to be absolutely patient and persistent to reap the benefits. Soft skills should be a way of life—and should not be looked upon as a 'use and throw' mechanism to achieve some desired short-term goal to be dumped later.

(*Source: The Ace of Soft Skills*, by Gopalaswamy Ramesh and Mahadevan Ramesh)

***Shylock:** A character from William Shakespeare's play,* The Merchant of Venice. *He is known for his greed and feelings of vengeance towards his enemies.*

Culture

Exercise 1

Answer the following in brief:

a. What does the writer mean by 'taking stock'?

b. How are soft skills related to each other?

c. Is it possible to develop too many skills at the same time?

d. Explain the saying, 'A ship is safest in the harbour, but that is not what it was designed for.'

Dictionary Work

Find out and write the meanings of the following words with the help of your dictionary. Work in pairs:

- Assiduously: ______
- Have one's antennae up: ______
- Introspection: ______
- Vengefulness: ______
- Arduous: ______
- Instant gratification: ______

Presentation

Go to the website: *http://en.wikipedia.org/wiki/Soft_skills*. Based on the various features on soft skills, do a presentation for your class.

PRONUNCIATION PRACTICE

Hotel Names and Other Words

Practise pronouncing the following words:

- The Ritz
- The Hyatt
- A-Loft
- Dallas
- Marriott Courtyards
- Hilton's Home
- Kiosk
- Reception
- Lobby

APPRECIATING LITERATURE

Presentation

Make a list of the world's most famous luxury hotels. Make a presentation on any one of your choice.

Reading

Read the following story by Saki, and answer the questions based on it:

The Phantom Luncheon

By *Saki*

'The Smithly-Dubbs are in Town,' said Sir James. 'I wish you would show them some attention. Ask them to lunch with you at the Ritz or somewhere.'

'From the little I've seen of the Smithly-Dubbs I don't think I want to cultivate their acquaintance,' said Lady Drakmanton.

'They always work for us at election times,' said her husband; 'I don't suppose they influence very many votes, but they have an uncle who is on one of my ward committees, and another uncle speaks sometimes at some of our less important meetings. Those sort of people expect some return in the shape of hospitality.'

'Expect it!' exclaimed Lady Drakmanton; 'the Misses Smithly-Dubb do more than that; they almost demand it. They belong to my club, and hang about the lobby just about lunch-time, all three of them, with their tongues hanging out of their mouths and the six-course look in their eyes. If I were to breathe the word "lunch" they would hustle me into a taxi and scream "Ritz" or "Dieudonne's" to the driver before I knew what was happening.'

'All the same, I think you ought to ask them to a meal of some sort,' persisted Sir James.

'Why can't you take them on, Milly?' she asked, turning hopefully to her sister.

'I don't know them,' said Milly hastily.

'All the better; you can pass yourself off as me. People say that we are so alike that they can hardly tell us apart, and I've only spoken to these tiresome young women about twice in my life, at committee-rooms, and bowed to them in the club. Any of the club page-boys will point them out to you; they're always to be found lolling about the hall just before lunch-time.'

'My dear Betty, don't be absurd,' protested Milly; 'I've got some people lunching with me at the Carlton tomorrow, and I'm leaving Town the day afterwards.'

'What time is your lunch tomorrow?' asked Lady Drakmanton reflectively.

'Two o'clock,' said Milly.

'Good,' said her sister; 'the Smithly-Dubbs shall lunch with me tomorrow. It shall be rather an amusing lunch-party. At least, I shall be amused.'

The last two remarks she made to herself. Other people did not always appreciate her ideas of humour. Sir James never did.

The next day Lady Drakmanton made some marked variations in her usual toilet effects. She dressed her hair in an unaccustomed manner, and put on a hat that added to the transformation of her appearance. When she had made one or two minor alterations she was sufficiently unlike her usual smart self to produce some hesitation in the greeting which the Misses Smithly-Dubb bestowed on her in the club-lobby. She responded, however, with a readiness which set their doubts at rest.

'What is the Carlton like for lunching in? she asked breezily.

The restaurant received an enthusiastic recommendation from the three sisters.

'Let's go and lunch there, shall we?' she suggested, and in a few minutes' time the Smithly-Dubb mind was contemplating at close quarters a happy vista of baked meats and approved vintage.

'Are you going to start with caviar? I am,' confided Lady Drakmanton, and the Smithly-Dubbs started with caviar. The subsequent dishes were chosen in the same spirit, and by the time they had arrived at the wild duck course it was beginning to be a rather expensive lunch.

The conversation hardly kept pace with the brilliancy of the menu. Repeated references on the part of the guests to the local political conditions and prospects in Sir James's constituency were met with vague 'ahs' and 'indeeds' from Lady Drakmanton, who might have been expected to be especially interested.

'I think when the Insurance Act is a little better understood it will lose some of its present unpopularity,' hazarded Cecilia Smithly-Dubb.

'Will it? I dare say. I'm afraid politics don't interest me very much,' said Lady Drakmanton.

The three Miss Smithly-Dubbs put down their cups of Turkish coffee and stared. Then they broke into protesting giggles.

'Of course, you're joking,' they said.

'Not me,' was the answer; 'I can't make head or tail of politics. Never could, and never want to. I've quite enough to do to manage my own affairs, and that's a fact.'

'But,' exclaimed Amanda Smithly-Dubb, with a squeal of bewilderment breaking into her voice, 'I was told you spoke so informingly about the Insurance Act at one of our social evenings.'

It was Lady Drakmanton who stared now. 'Do you know,' she said, with a scared look around her, 'rather a dreadful thing is happening. I'm suffering from a complete loss of memory. I can't even think who I am. I remember meeting you somewhere, and I remember you asking me to come and lunch with you here, and that I accepted your kind invitation. Beyond that my mind is a positive blank.'

'You asked us to lunch,' her companions exclaimed hurriedly. That seemed a more immediately important point to clear up than the question of identity.

'Oh, no,' said the vanishing hostess, 'That I do remember about. You insisted on my coming here because the feeding was so good, and I must say it comes up to all you said about it. A very nice lunch it's been. What I'm worrying about is who on earth am I? I haven't the faintest notion?'

'You are Lady Drakmanton,' exclaimed the three sisters in chorus.

'Now, don't make fun of me,' she replied, crossly, 'I happen to know her quite well by sight, and she isn't a bit like me. And it's an odd thing you should have mentioned her, for it so happens she's just come into the room. That lady in black, with the yellow plume in her hat, there over by the door.'

The Smithly-Dubbs looked in the indicated direction, and the uneasiness in their eyes deepened into horror. In outward appearance the lady who had just entered the room certainly came rather nearer to their recollection of their Member's wife than the individual who was sitting at table with them.

'Who are you, then, if that is Lady Drakmanton?' they asked in panic-stricken bewilderment.

'That is just what I don't know,' was the answer; 'and you don't seem to know much better than I do.'

'You came up to us in the club –'

'In what club?'

'The New Didactic, in Calais Street.'

'The New Didactic!' exclaimed Lady Drakmanton with an air of returning illumination; 'thank you so much. Of course, I remember now who I am. I'm Ellen Niggle, of the Ladies' Brasspolishing Guild. The Club employs me to come now and then and see to the polishing of the brass fittings. That's how I came to know Lady Drakmanton by sight; she's very often in the Club. And you are the ladies who so kindly asked me out to lunch. Funny how it should all have slipped my memory, all of a sudden. The unaccustomed good food and wine must have been too much for me; for the moment I really couldn't call to mind who I was. Good gracious,' she broke off suddenly, 'it's ten past two; I should be at a polishing job in Whitehall. I must scuttle off like a giddy rabbit. Thanking you ever so.'

She left the room with a scuttle sufficiently suggestive of the animal she had mentioned, but the giddiness was all on the side of her involuntary hostesses. The restaurant seemed to be spinning round them; and the bill when it appeared did nothing to restore their composure. They were as nearly in tears as it is permissible to be during the luncheon hour in a really good restaurant. Financially speaking, they were well able to afford the luxury of an elaborate lunch, but their ideas on the subject of entertaining differed very sharply, according to the circumstances of whether they were dispensing or receiving hospitality. The Smithly-Dubbs never quite recovered from their experience. They have given up politics and taken to doing good.

The Ritz, Dieudonne's, Carlton: All premier luxury hotels with branches all over the world.

Culture

Exercise 1

Answer the following questions.

i. What is a phantom? How appropriate is the title of the story?

____

____

____

____

ii. Who is Sir James? Why does he want his wife to entertain the Smithly-Dubbs sisters?

____

____

____

____

iii. What role did Lady Drakmanton's sister play in the story?

____

____

____

____

Essential Vocabulary

Go through the meanings of the following expressions:

- **Marked variations:** noticeable changes
- **Crossly:** in a bad temper
- **Breezily:** lightly, good-humouredly
- **Illumination:** (here) recollection
- **Bewildered:** Confused, mildly angry
- **Scuttle off like a giddy rabbit:** leave in a hurry
- **Vague:** unclear

Exercise 1

Fill in the blanks with the appropriate words from those given above:

i. The response was very ____________; I couldn't follow it at all.
ii. After the party, the children ____________.
iii. The food was unappreciated and the manager looked at the chef ____________.
iv. After the renovation, there are some ____________ in the hotel.
v. The staff was ____________ by the behaviour of the strange guest.

Discussion

Describe a typical six-course lunch in your hotel.

10

SOLVING GUESTS' PROBLEMS

In This Unit

Situation
- Assisting the guest during an emergency

Grammar Bin
- Phrasal verbs

Language Focus
- Responding to queries and complaints

Reading Comprehension
- The Vigeland Park

Real-life Reads
- Advertisements

Workplace Skills
- Presentation

Pronunciation Practice
- Kitchen words

SITUATION

Assisting the Guest During an Emergency

Discussion

What are the problems which one can have with a hotel guest? Did you ever have a problem in a hotel? Discuss what happened and how you managed the situation with your partner. Use the words given below to describe your problem.

People in a Hotel

- Waiter
- Bell boy
- Receptionist
- Travel agent
- Hotel general manager
- Restaurant manager

Now read and practise the following conversation describing an emergency situation.

Receptionist: Good morning. Reception. How may I help you?
Guest: I'm calling from room 685. I have a flight to Delhi at 11 am and I've lost my handbag. My air ticket was in it.
Receptionist: I'm sorry to hear about that, madam. Would you like me to connect you to the travel agency?
Guest: Could you do that? It's already 8 o'clock and I don't want to miss my flight.
Receptionist: Please don't worry madam, we'll do our best to sort this out.
Guest: Thank you so much.
Receptionist: You're welcome, madam. Our agent will contact you shortly with details of all the available flights.

Read and practise the following conversation, which describes another emergency situation which a guest might face in a hotel.

Guest: Hello. Reception?
Receptionist: Good afternoon. What can I do for you, sir?
Guest: I'm from room 321. I can't turn off the taps in the washbasin. They are stuck and the basin is about to overflow.
Receptionist: We are extremely sorry for the inconvenience, sir. I'll inform the duty manager on your floor. It'll soon be taken care of. Someone would be in your room within a couple of minutes to correct it.
Guest: I'm very annoyed with your hotel management. These things should be taken care of before you allot rooms to guests.
Receptionist: I'm extremely sorry, sir. We'll fix the problem immediately.
Guest: Alright.

Exercise 1

Fill in the blanks using the following expressions. These expressions use common verbs to explain how things work.

Turn on	Switch off	Select
Turn off	Surf	Order

i. I would like to watch some TV; please could you ____________ the set?
ii. The menu is in the drawer on the right hand, you may please ____________ any of the items.
iii. Please could you ____________ the dressing table lights; they are too harsh.
iv. I would like to ____________ a plate of penne pasta.
v. Could you get me the remote please, I want to ____________ channels.

Exercise 2

Imagine that you are working in a hotel. Reflect upon a recent time when you had difficulty in coping with a client. Consider the following, and make notes in the following space:

- What was the situation?
- Who did you have difficulty with?
- What did you do about the situation?
- Were you satisfied with the way you handled the situation?

____

____

____

____

____

____

GRAMMAR BIN

Phrasal Verbs

Phrasal verbs are verbs that consist of two or sometimes three words, where the first word is a verb which is followed by an adverb or a preposition or both.

Given below are a few phrasal verbs, with their meanings. Read through them carefully.

i. **Rush (something) out:** To produce something very quickly.
ii. **Put yourself out:** To make a special effort to do something for somebody
iii. **Take after:** To look or behave like an older member of the family; also, to follow somebody quickly.
iv. **Work somebody over:** To attack somebody and hit them.
v. **To key somebody for something:** To make something or somebody suitable for a particular purpose.
vi. **Visit with somebody:** To spend time with somebody.

vii. **Wait on:** To wait for something to happen before one does or decides something.
viii. **Go with:** Agree with.
ix. **Roll down:** put down.
x. **Sold on to:** Committed to.

Exercise 1

Fill in the blanks with the appropriate phrasal verbs from the list given above:

i. Susie ____________ Sunny because she wanted to be the first one to tell him the news.
ii. He has not ____________ his aunt in the old age home for a long time.
iii. It's so stuffy in here, please ____________ the window of the car.
iv. Danny and Blessy ____________ Joe ____________ to get the truth out of him.
v. The Khannas are completely ____________ the idea of starting a restaurant.
vi. The crew has to ____________ the captain's decisions.

What not to do when dining in a restaurant!

- *Slouching*
- *Fidgeting*
- *Smacking your lips*
- *Crunching*
- *Touching your face or hair*
- *Blowing your nose*
- *Chewing with your mouth open*
- *Talking with your mouth full*
- *Pushing away your plate when finished*
- *Picking or flossing your teeth*

Culture

LANGUAGE FOCUS

Responding to Queries and Complaints

Here are a few things to say when you are faced with complaints or problems:

- Is there anything I can do?
- Would you like me to?
- What I suggest you do is….

Note the following conversations between clients and a staff member. How would you respond in a similar situation? Would you respond in the same way, or would you handle the situation differently? Write your response in the space provided.

i. My key is not working.

a. Let me take a look at it.

____

____

ii. Can you send my order to my room fast?

a. We're doing our best.

____

____

iii. I would like to have a discount on the suite.

a. Our hotel doesn't give discounts.

____

____

iv. How do we get to the hotel from the airport?

a. It's close. You can walk down.

____

____

v. My cell phone is missing. I think the room service boy stole it.

a. I don't believe you.

____

____

READING COMPREHENSION

Pre-reading Activity

Is there a museum or a famous park in your town/city? Tell your group about it.

Reading

Read the following passage.

The Vigeland Park

The Vigeland Park is the world‘s largest sculpture park made by a single artist, and is one of Norway‘s most popular tourist attractions. The park is open to visitors all year round.

The unique sculpture park is Gustav Vigeland‘s lifework with more than 200 sculptures in bronze, granite and wrought iron. Vigeland was also in-charge of the design and architectural layout of the park. The Vigeland Park was mainly completed between 1939 and 1949. Most of the sculptures are placed in five units along an 850 meter long axis: The Main gate, the Bridge with the Children's playground, the Fountain, the Monolith plateau and the Wheel of Life.

The construction work in what was to become the Vigeland park lasted for many years. The area east of the pond had been a public park since the turn of the 20th century. In 1924, it was decided that Vigeland‘s Fountain and Monolith with surrounding granite groups were to be erected on a large area west of the pond. In 1931, Vigeland‘s park plan, including the bridge decorated with sculptures, was approved by the City Council. The magnificent main gate, which was financed by Oslo Sparebank, had already been approved in 1927.

The Vigeland Park was mainly completed between 1939 and 1949. The City of Oslo was its main contributor, but a number of private persons and companies also contributed. All the sculptures in the Vigeland Park were modelled in full size in clay by Gustav Vigeland. He then let professional craftsmen do the carving in granite and casting in bronze. Vigeland was also in charge of the design and architectural layout of the vast area of 80 acres.

The Bridge

The 100 m long and 15 m wide bridge, lined with lanterns and sculptures on the granite parapets, is built on top of an old bridge constructed in 1914. Vigeland designed the new bridge and modelled in the years 1925 to 1933, the 58 sculptures in bronze. These include a rich variety of children, women and men in different ages, some alone, others in groups. Dominant motifs are the relationships between man and woman, adults and children. Stationary figures that flank the cube formed lanterns alternate with dynamic groups. By the run of the waterfall, the bridge widens to each side and is marked with figures surrounded by massive bronze wheels. Here you will also find Sinnataggen, the little Angry Boy.

In spite of his size, the little boy is one of the most popular figures in the park. Although the sculptures on the bridge were among the latest Vigeland made for the park, they were the first to be installed. Already in the summer of 1940, when the rest of the park still was a large construction area, the bridge was opened to the public. At this time, the four tall granite columns portraying humans fighting lizards were also erected. These show demons in absolute control of their victims and represent a dramatic contrast to the more unconcerned play and joy of life depicted on the bridge.

Below the bridge is a circular playground with eight bronze sculptures of small children. In the centre, mounted on a small granite column, is the figure of an unborn child. Vigeland also designed a children's ferry to the amusement of the park's younger visitors, and the boat had its monumental granite wharf a few steps further down from the Children's Playground. For many years, after the Second World War, it sailed around where today only swans and ducks swim. Inspired by other public parks in Europe, Vigeland also wanted rowing boats in the upper pond. This plan was, however, never carried out. Some sculptures are placed outside the main axis in the Vigeland Park.

At the end of an axis that intersect the main axis in north, is Vigeland's monumental bronze group the Clan (1934–36). With the exception of the Monolith, this group is Vigeland's largest sculpture and consists of 21 figures. The original model in plaster was stored in the Vigeland Museum until 1985, when a gift from IBM made it possible to have it cast in bronze and erected in the park in 1988, according to Vigeland's original plan.

On the opposite side of the main axis, is the two sculptures: Young girl kneeling, encircled by a coiled lizard (1938) and Young boy and girl leaning against each other over a well (1939). Near the Vigeland Museum to the south, the Triangle (1938) is placed on a circular extension in the diagonal path leading from the Monolith.

To the north inside the Main Entrance stands Vigeland's self-portrait (1942). Dressed in his everyday working clothes, with hammer and chisel in hand, he stands as a signature of his own work.

(Adapted from: *http://www.vigeland.museum.no/en/vigeland-park/*)

Exercise 1

Answer the following questions.

i. What is unique about the Vigeland Park?

____

____

ii. Name the five units of the park.

____

____

iii. Describe Vigeland's self-portrait.

____

____

____

Exercise 2

Complete the following sentences with appropriate words and expressions from the passage:

i. ____________ was the main contributor for the Vigeland Park.
ii. In spite of his size, the ____________ is one of the most popular figures in the park.
iii. Dominant motifs in the park are the relationships ____________.
iv. Sculptures in the park are made of bronze, granite and ____________.

Exercise 3

Give one word for the following:

i. A huge or impressive achievement: ____________
ii. A decorative applique design or figure, as of lace or velvet, used in trimming: ____________
iii. A landing place that usually comprises a fixed platform, often on pilings: ____________

REAL-LIFE READS

Advertisements

Reading

Read the following advertisement and answer the questions that follow:

Advertisements

Hotel Delight

A Unique Luxury Business Hotel

Hotel Delight, a landmark business hotel that spells luxury and comfort, whether you are here on business or holiday.

A blend of the traditional and contemporary, Hotel Delight is the epitome of style and luxury and stands tall in the heart of the historical city of Jaipur. We offer 46 rooms and suites, befitting a luxury hotel; the rooms are designed with space, elegance and luxury. The highlight of our rooms are:

- Mini refrigerator with refreshments
- Working desk with ergonomic chair
- Satellite TV with Indian and International channels
- Tea and coffee making facilities
- Telephone with domestic direct dialling

- Iron and ironing board
- Centralized and individual climate control
- Wired and wireless Internet access
- Cozy beds with duvet/blankets
- Black-out curtain
- Well-appointed bathroom

Royal Court

With its plush décor, Royal Court has a rich variety that includes multi-cuisine delicacies, buffet and a la carte, which will invariably excite your taste buds.

Café de Royale

This coffee bar has an ambience par excellence. Share cups of steaming coffee or have conversation over hot snacks.

Regal Court

It has a vintage look with antique furniture and wood décor.

Banqueting and Conferencing

The halls are designed to carry out any occasion and event conveniently. From a small board meeting to a big conference, birthday parties to weddings, we offer a perfect venue. With rooms that can accommodate as few as 20, or halls enough for even a 1000 people, we provide a wide variety to our patrons.

We also provide: Round-the-clock room service, safe lockers, currency exchange, in-house laundry, doctor on call and a lot more.

In and around Jaipur

Our travel desk also assists and provides customized tour packages on request.

Exercise 1

In a group, prepare a brochure for circulation for your hotel. Follow the model used above.

Exercise 2

Answer the following in brief:

a. What are the room facilities available in Hotel Delight?

____

____

____

b. Describe the features of the dining halls and café in Hotel Delight.

____

____

____

c. What are some of the additional facilities that the hotel provides?

____

____

____

Exercise 3

Fill in the blanks using the words given below:

landmark	well-appointed	antique	ambience	steaming

a. They live in a luxurious and ____________ flat.
b. This shop deals in ____________ furniture.
c. The Flora Building is a well-known ____________ of our city.
d. The aroma of ____________ rice is so delightful.
e. They did not like the hotel because of its ____________.

Dictionary Work

Find out the meanings of the following words. You can work in pairs:

- Ergonomic: ____________
- Vintage: ____________
- Epitome: ____________
- Plush: ____________
- Customized: ____________

WORKPLACE SKILLS

Presentation

Make a presentation in groups describing the people of your city. You should mention:

- if they are friendly/unfriendly;
- what work/occupations are popular among them;
- what you like or dislike about them

The presentation should be professionally made, using PowerPoint and should include pictures and charts. Try to make your presentation as appealing as possible.

PRONUNCIATION PRACTICE

Kitchen Words

Practise the pronunciation of the following words:

Overcooked	Attendant	Duplicate
Heating	Reservation	A la carte
Hygienic	Replacement	Table d'hôte

11

At the Restaurant

Situation
- Managing guests in the hotel restaurant
- Changing the order

Vocabulary
- Essential food vocabulary
- Are you being served?
- Restaurant menu

Writing
- Letter of complaint

Grammar Bin
- Food-related adjectives
- Verbs: make/do

Language Focus
- Expressing agreement with a statement
- Polite expressions

Speaking
- Guest and waiter

Pronunciation Practice
- Words related to dining

SITUATION

Managing Guests in the Hotel Restaurant

John and Reena Verghese are staying at a hotel and go for dinner to the hotel's restaurant. They meet the restaurant manager in the dining hall. Read and practise the following conversation with your partner.

Manager: Good evening. Welcome to the Neva.
John: Good evening. Can we have a table for two, please?
Manager: Of course, sir. Are you staying with us?
John: Yes. We are in room number 1106. John Verghese.
Manager: Please come this way. Would you like to have the corner table?
John: Excellent. Thank you. (*They sit*)
Waiter: Good evening Ma'am. Good evening, sir. I'm Joe. I'll be serving you this evening. May I bring you the menu, now?
John: Sure. I think we are *a tad* too early. There aren't too many people around.
Waiter: Well sir. The live band is here and a lot more guests shall be pouring in shortly. May I bring you the menu, now?
John: Yes, of course.
Reena: This is so *swanky*.
John: It is. I've heard that it is a wonderful band.
Waiter: Our menu, Ma'am. Sir. I shall be back in a little while for the orders.
John: Thank you. (To Reena) Would you like to have a look at the menu?
Reena: Sure, I'm *starving*.
John: Waiter, may we have another menu, please? Thank you. We shall place an order in a moment.
Reena: Hmmm, chicken *barbequed*, chicken *fricasséed, steak*. And what have they got for seafood? Swordfish, prawns and lobsters!
John: Let's begin with something to drink along with *starters*.
Waiter: May I have your beverage order please?
John: Yes. A Gimlet for the lady and I'll have a regular scotch on-the-rocks.
Waiter: Certainly sir. Would you prefer a Ballantine or a Red Label?
John: A single Ballantine. And also some Assorted Non-vegetarian Deluxe Canapés.
Waiter: Right, Sir. A Gimlet for Ma'am, a single Ballantine on-the-rocks for you and a portion of Assorted Non-vegetarian Deluxe Canapes.
John: Yes, that's right.
Waiter: Thank you. I shall be back for the food orders later.
… …
Waiter: A portion of Assorted Non-vegetarian Deluxe Canapes. The Gimlet for you Ma'am. How many cubes of ice would you like in your single Ballantine on-the-rocks, sir?
John: Oh, just fill up the glass.
Waiter: Certainly, Sir. Would you like to place the order for the food now or, shall I come back later?
John: Yeah. We shall start with *appetizers* and bread sticks.

Waiter: Right away sir. Would you like to order some soup? I'd recommend the French onion soup, that's the *specialty* of our restaurant.
Reena: I'd like to try that out.
John: For me, one Scotch *broth,* please.
Waiter: Very well. And how would you like your salad?
John: Do you have any suggestions?
Waiter: I'd suggest Caesar *salad with vinaigrette dressing.*
John: All right, we'll go for it.
Reena: Can we have a *lo-cal* dressing, please?
Waiter: Certainly. May I take your order for the main dishes?
John: Umm, we haven't figured out what we want yet. What would you suggest?
Waiter: If I may recommend, the steaks and lobsters are excellent tonight. And you must try our sauce, La Temptation, our *chef's* specialty.
John: Is that really so? Then we shall have it, along with some *veal* and *lobsters.*
Waiter: Right away, sir. How would you like the steak—rare, medium or well done?
John: Well done, please.
Waiter: Let me repeat your order, sir.

Remember!

- *The waiter must repeat the order before he leaves the table.*
- *There are two options for the order for desserts to be taken—the guest has the option of either ordering the dessert while ordering the main course or after the main course is 'cleared'.*

Changing the Order

A guest at the restaurant might ask you to change their order. Read and practise the following conversation with your partner.

John: Could I change my order? I would like two fruit cocktails first.
Waiter: Two fruit cocktails? Very well, sir.
John: Will it take too long?
Waiter: Not at all sir. Just give us a couple of minutes.
John: That's fine. Thank you.
Waiter: And would you like to drink mineral or regular water?
John: A bottle of sparkling mineral water, please.

VOCABULARY

Go through the following words and their meanings.

Table 11.1 Food Words

WORD	MEANING
Tad	(Informal) a very slight amount or degree.
Swanky	High-class, very stylish and expensive.
Starving	(Here, informal) Very hungry.
Chicken Barbequed	(Here) Chicken cooked on the barbecue, taken with a special sauce.
Fricasséed	Meat sliced and fried or stewed and served with sauce.
Steak	A thick slice of any type of meat.
Starters	A small amount of food that is served before the main course of a meal. This usage is mainly British, but is found in American English as well. The Americans prefer to call it 'appetizers.'
Appetizers	Please see above.
Dips	A crisp and salty biscuit in the shape of a stick. You can dip it in soup or butter, depending on your calorie consciousness.
Pretzels	A crisp salty biscuit in the shape of a knot or stick, often served with drinks at a party.
Specialty	This is an American spelling. In British English, you would find it spelt as speciality. It refers to a type of food or product that a restaurant is famous for because it is very good.
Broth	A thick soup made by boiling meat or fish and vegetables in water. Chicken broth is supposedly very popular and nutritious.
Salad with dressing	A thin sauce used to add flavour to salads, usually made from oil, vinegar salt, salt, pepper, etc. The expression has found its way into the American usage, however, they also use the term *stuffing*.
Lo-cal	(Informal) It means low calorie. When you ask for something lo-cal, it means you are very weight (and figure/health) conscious.
Chef	A professional cook, especially the senior most cook in a restaurant, hotel, etc.
Veal	Meat from a calf, or a young cow.
Lobster	A sea creature with a hard shell, a long body divided into sections and two large claws. Lobster's meat is an extremely expensive delicacy.

Exercise 1

Use the words given in the above list and fill in the blanks:

1. This Diet Cola is very ___________, you won't put on weight by drinking this.
2. This hotel has a great ___________.
3. Caramel custard is a ___________ of this restaurant.
4. I don't need any ___________, I'll go straight for the main course.
5. Drink this ___________ You need energy after a long illness.

Are You Being Served?

We know that in a *buffet*, people serve themselves from a table; on the other hand, in an *à la carte* we choose from a list of dishes that have separate prices, as we see in the above situation. But what do we call the service that takes place after ordering *à la carte*? Go through the following table:

Table 11.2 Styles of Serving in a Restaurant

SERVICE	HOW IT WORKS	COMMON IN INDIA?
Russian	The food is first shown around the table. The waiter serves the food from a serving dish, using a serving spoon and fork.	Very occasionally
Silver (Also called English service)	The waiter serves the food at a table from a serving dish, using a serving spoon and fork.	Frequently
French	Partially cooked food is brought from the kitchen on a cart which is used also for the final cooking. Food is completed in front of the guests and served by a waiter or waitress who offers a dish to each guest who helps himself or herself.	Not common
Plated	The food is put on the individual plates in the kitchen	Quite common
Family	All the food is served in serving dishes that are placed on the table so that the guests can help themselves.	Most common
Gueridon	The waiter carves, or cooks at a 'Gueridon' trolley and then places the food on to the plate which is placed before the guest.	Sometimes
Mixed	The main course is put on a plate in the kitchen and the side dishes are put on the table in serving dishes so that the guests can help themselves.	Sometimes
American	Particularly suited to banquets. All the glass and silver, plus napkin and a service plate are on the table when the guest arrives.	Occasionally

Restaurant Menu

Exercise 1

Given below is the outline of the menu of The Piano restaurant. Using the following list, fill in the menu in the appropriate sections. Look up the meanings in the dictionary if necessary.

Chicken   Turkey   Chef's Pates   Zucchini   Broccoli

Sweet corn chowder cobblers prawn and orange cocktail cottage cheese Lentils sherbet jambalaya mousse asparagus shrimp bisque Ham Caesar salad Scotch broth pretzels steak okra potato Croquettes soufflé lima beans catfish muffins Gumbos vichyssoise herring and apple salad Russian salad

Remember these pointers about menus:

- Appetizers are called hors d'oeuvres in French
- Remember to include a few salads in the appetizers
- Soups can also be called potage
- Main courses are of two kinds: the entrée and the remove/releve, the latter being the heavier and more important one

Menu

The Piano

Hors d'oeuvres

Soups

Non-Vegetarian Main Course

Entrée

Vegetarian Side Dishes

Desserts

____________	____________	____________
____________	____________	____________

WRITING

Letter of Complaint

On the recommendation of his friend John Verghese, Atul Bannerjee, Sales Manager at a reputed company, visits the restaurant, Le Maxim with his clients. However, he is extremely disappointed with the service and writes a letter of complaint to the restaurant manager. Read the letter, given here.

7 September 2012

To,
The Manager
Le Maxim
Hastings Street
Kolkata

Dear Sir

Last evening, I had invited six of my clients to join me for dinner at your restaurant, recommended to me by my friend. But I regret to say that the service was deplorable, although the food was pretty good.

I had made a reservation for the 'Smoking' section. However, there was some confusion and we were given the 'Non-smoking' corner, instead. Next, the server took his own time between courses. I'm sure you would agree that such long gaps between courses kill the appetite. And the final embarrassment was when my credit card was declared expired, in front of my guests. Later, it was found that it was a computer error.

This is not at all professional by any standard. I hope that this does not happen again.

Sincerely,
Atul Bannerjee

Exercise 1

As the manager of Le Maxim, write a response to Mr Bannerjee's letter of complaint in the space provided.

GRAMMAR BIN

Food-related Adjectives

We know adjectives are words that modify or add something to the noun. In other words, an adjective describes a noun. For example, we can have a dessert which is 'rich', 'light' and 'tangy'. Similarly, we can have sauces that are 'savoury, 'creamy' or 'spicy'.

Some other ways to describe food are by using the following adjectives:

- Sweet (with sugar or sweetener)
- Bland (which does not have enough taste)
- Salty (a lot of salt)
- Savoury (pleasant)
- Overcooked (cooked too much)
- Rich (with a lot of butter, fat, eggs, etc.)
- Creamy (containing a lot of cream
- Tangy (a strong, sharp taste or smell)
- Seasoned (with added spices/salt/pepper)

Exercise 1

Can you find adjectives to describe the following?

Soup	Salad	Bread
Curry	Pie	Pizza

Verbs: Make/Do

Read the following sentence:
'I made a reservation last week.'
Here, the verb *make* is used to mean *setting up* something.

Do and *make* are both action verbs. *Make* can be used in the following ways:
They *made* a huge profit.
He *makes* great music.
Yusuf *makes* the best cakes in town.
Would you like *to make* a call to your parents?

Here are some expressions with *make: Make reservations, make arrangement, make an effort, make merry, make an excuse, make money, make mistakes, make a mess, make a fuss, make a noise, make progress, make a speech, make trouble, make up one's mind.*

Exercise 1

Complete the following sentences using expressions with make. Use a dictionary if necessary.

1. Mary's grades are improving and she ____________.
2. You are confused about selecting your courses. You must ____________.
3. His business is doing very well and he ____________.
4. Anita never admits to her mistakes and is always ____________ to cover them up.
5. If you seriously ____________, you are sure to succeed.
6. They tip-toed in, without ____________.

The verb *do* can be used in the following ways:

- What does he do? (What's his job?)
- I don't want any lunch. A cup of coffee will do. (Will be sufficient)
- She cannot do without her iPod. (always needs)
- Your brother is here. It's something to do with your car. (connected with)
- I've done my room. (cleaned)
- Don't do drugs. (try)

Here are some more expressions with *do: Do your best, do business (with someone), do a course, do someone a favour, do good, do harm, do harm, do-it-yourself, do well.*

Exercise 2

Complete the following sentences with the above expressions:

1. She has ____________ her friends many ____________ yet they did not come forward to help her when she needed them.
2. Try this ____________ kit. It makes painting your house very easy.

3. He is reliable and honest. We would love to ___________ with him.
4. She needs to ___________ in anger management.
5. I am surprised to learn that he ___________ in the exam.

Exercise 3

Fill in the blanks with the correct form of *make* or *do*.

1. Niki will pass the exams, but she would not ___________ it to the top.
2. I always try to ___________ my best, whenever I am given a responsibility.
3. Who shall I ___________ the check out to?
4. The police has ___________ no progress in investigating the case.
5. The government has ___________ extra provisions against bad crop this year.
6. His business is ___________ well, and he has ___________ lots of money.
7. You need to ___________ away with all these regulations if you want better results.
8. I can ___________ with a computer of my own.
9. Could you ___________ me a favour, please?
10. The new project will ___________ more demands on my time.

LANGUAGE FOCUS

Expressing Agreement With a Statement

Read the following exchange.

> **John:** I've a reservation with you.
> **Manager:** Of course, sir.

Here, we see how the manager expresses agreement with the customer's statement. In our day to day conversation, too, we need to choose the right word or phrase to suggest that we agree with the speaker. We express agreement with a speaker in various ways. Some of these expressions are:

- Undoubtedly
- Sure
- I agree (with you)
- Exactly
- Quite right
- Absolutely
- Certainly
- Positively

Exercise 1

Use the above expressions to fill in the blanks given below. One has been done for you.

Let's go for a walk.
Sure.

1. I always felt that Hari is very dishonest.

 ____

2. This is not the kind of weather in which we should be going out.

 ____

3. We ought to report the matter to the police.

 ____

4. Haley is the most beautiful girl in our class.

 ____

5. I am certain that Amit would help us.

 ____

6. We shall reach Hyderabad by 10 am.

 ____

Polite Expressions

Go through the following expressions of politeness and their meanings.

Table 11.3 Expressions of Politeness

EXPRESSIONS	SIGNIFICANCE
Good Morning	To greet somebody between the early hours of morning till before 12 pm.
Good Evening	To wish someone after 3 pm.
Good Night	To greet someone before taking their leave at night.
Thank you	To express thanks over a kind act, on receiving a gift, an information, or a compliment. (Example: 'You look good' or 'You keep your house very well.')
Sorry	Apologizing for a rude action or word, whether intended or not. It is also used to express regret over something.
Excuse me	To interrupt someone who is speaking, to request someone to make way for you. Also to suggest that you are sorry to disturb somebody.

Exercise 1

Fill in the blanks with right expressions:

1. ____________ for calling. How can I help you?
2. ____________ aren't you a student of Loyola College?
3. ____________, without this information I would not have been able to reach a decision.
4. ____________ for calling you at this late hour, but this is rather important.
5. ____________, viewers. These are the news headlines. (10 pm at night)

SPEAKING

Guest and Waiter

You are at a restaurant with a friend. Place your order with the waiter. You may use the following list of words in your conversation:

Salads	Shrimp Cocktail	Appetizers
Melon	Potatoes Spinach	Corn
Lobsters	Tomato Juice	String Beans Vegetables

PRONUNCIATION PRACTICE

Words Related to Dining

Restaurant	Salad	Menu
Server	Barbecued	Fricasseed
Appetizers	Pretzels	Specialty
Chef		

12

PLACES TO VISIT IN THE CITY

Situation
- Talking to guests about places in the city
- At the travel desk

Speaking
- Talking about places of attraction in the city
- Discussion

Vocabulary
- Talking about the weather
- Weather-related idioms and colloquial expressions

Grammar Bin
- Question tags

Writing
- Dialogues
- Varieties of food

Language Focus
- Presentations
- Idioms and expressions related to food

Real-life Reads
- About Hotel Regency

Appreciating Literature
- *A Room with a View* by E.M. Forster

Pronunciation Practice
- Places in the hotel

SITUATION

Talking to Guests About Places in the City

Stuart Moy is an American businessman travelling to Indore. He wants to explore the city and the places around it and approaches the reception desk. Read and practise the following conversation.

Receptionist: Good morning, sir. Hope you slept well last night.
Guest: I did, thank you.
Receptionist: How may I help you, sir?
Guest: We would like to go for some sightseeing today. Could you suggest some places of historical interest?
Receptionist: Certainly, sir. Allow me to refer you to the travel desk.

Read and practise the conversation between the guest and the receptionist after the former returns from his sightseeing trip:

Receptionist: Good evening, sir? How was your visit to the museum?
Guest: It was good, thank you; it's a lovely place.
Receptionist: It is indeed, sir. Hope the car journey was comfortable?
Guest: Not really; it was quite tiring. But the trip was worth it.
Receptionist: I'm glad you enjoyed the trip. Please let us know if you would like us to arrange for a different car the next time. Can I send some refreshments for you?
Guest: That would be great. I'd like to have some coffee, please.
Receptionist: Certainly, sir. I'll ask the room service to do so.

At the Travel Desk

Read and practise the following conversation between a guest and a travel agent at the hotel.

Travel Agent: Would you be interested in forts and castles, sir? We have a number of those here, all very popular with tourists.
Guest: Sounds good. Is it possible to have some details about the castles?
Travel Agent: Sure, sir. Here's the city guide, with all the details of our major attractions. May I recommend Fort Royale? It is little far from the city but well worth the trip.
Travel Agent: I see. Alright, let me take a look at this guide.
Travel Agent: Would you like the hotel to arrange for a cab, sir?
Guest: Sure, how does the travel agency charge?
Travel Agent: Here's the fare list, sir. And may I offer you the brochure containing all the additional information about the city?
Guest: Thank you.
Travel Agent: You're welcome, sir. Hope you enjoy your sightseeing.

SPEAKING

Talking About Places of Attraction in the City

Tell a client about some major places of attractions in your city. Take turns in playing the role of the receptionist and the guest. Your talk may include:

- Theme parks
- Art galleries and museums
- Monuments
- Markets
- Beaches/mountains

Discussion

Which time of the year is the best time for tourists to visit your country? Discuss.

VOCABULARY

Talking About the Weather

Here is a list of words you need to know about the weather.

Table 12.1 Weather Words

WIND	RAIN	COLD	HOT	MIST
Breeze	Drizzle	Chilly	Scorching	Fog
Wind	Shower	Frosty	Boiling	Haze
Blustery	Downpour	Sleet	Humid	Smog
Gale	Damp	Slush	Heat wave	
Hurricane	Torrential rain	Snowdrifts	Drought	
Cyclone	Overcast			
Typhoon	Hailstones			
Squall	Monsoon			
Tornado (Twister)				
Whirlwind				

Exercise 1

Fill in the blanks using the words given in the above list:

i. Switch on the air conditioner, it's ____________ hot today.
ii. The visibility is poor when one is driving through a thick ____________.
iii. With temperature shooting up to 49, there was a ____________.
iv. There is a gentle ____________ .on the beach. Shall we go for a walk?
v. The white snow has turned into dirty ____________.

vi. I could feel the ____________ hitting our roof.
vii. ____________ Susie is fast approaching the coasts.
viii. If it does not rain, we'll have the worst ____________ in a decade.
ix. The ____________ blew my hat in an instant.
x. If the heavy ____________ continues, we'll have a flood.

Weather-related Idioms and Colloquial Expressions

i. **To get into hot weather:** To be or get into trouble.
ii. **To be hot on somebody's heels:** To follow someone closely.
iii. **To get hot under the collar:** To get angry.
iv. **To be in the hot seat:** To take responsibility for an important or difficult decision.
v. **To get cold feet:** To suddenly become nervous about doing something that one was planning to do.
vi. **To leave somebody out in the cold:** To not include someone in a group or activity.
vii. **When it rains, it pours (British or Indian English version: it never rains but it pours):** When one bad thing happens, other bad things follow.
viii. **To rain on somebody's parade:** To spoil something for somebody.
ix. **Take a rain check on something:** To refuse an invitation but say that you may accept it later

Exercise 1
Fill in the blanks using the expressions given before.

i. John did not complete the work, and now he has got himself into ____________.
ii. The manager is extremely____________ today because of yesterday's trouble with the banquet.
iii. Mary broke her leg, and next day her brother fractured his arm; truly ____________.
iv. She wanted to take a holiday but an emergency situation prevented her and ____________.
v. He wanted to quit his job, but got____________ at the last minute.

GRAMMAR BIN

Question Tags

Question tags are a common device in conversation, where one makes a statement and at once asks the listener to confirm it. It can be done in different ways. For example:

- He is coming, **isn't he**?
- She was rude, **wasn't she**?
- He is ambitious, **isn't he**?

We can make a negative statement with a **positive question tag**:

- They aren't home, **are they**?
- He isn't very clever, **is he**?
- She doesn't like pizza, **does she**?

Imperative Sentences (sentences giving orders) become polite requests when question tags are added. For example:

- Turn down the volume, will you?
- Let's go for a movie, shall we?
- You'd better talk to her, shouldn't you?

Exercise 1

Read the following sentences, and fill in the blanks using question tags.

i. They do come from a rather large family, ____________ ?
ii. This is a notable discovery, ____________?
iii. John does fancy Joanna, ____________?
iv. Hema isn't a very friendly person, ____________?
v. Dev doesn't like action movies, ____________?
vi. She is such a scatter-brain, ____________?
vii. I'm your leader, ____________?
viii. You can't possibly do that ____________?
ix. The Mehras weren't in town when this happened, ____________?
x. You would need the automobile, ____________?

Making Adjectives

Exercise 1

The word *secretarial* is formed by adding the suffix *-ial* to *secretary* and removing *y*. Make adjectives of the following words by adding *-ial*.

- Office: ________________________________
- Benefit: ________________________________
- Air: ________________________________
- Face: ________________________________
- Picture: ________________________________

Learn more about using adjectives from the following websites:

- *http://www.learn-english today.com/lessons/lesson_contents/adjectives-ex.html*
- *http://ebasics.blogspot.com/2008/06/vocabulary-adjectives-for-describing.html*
- *http://www.enchantedlearning.com/grammar/partsofspeech/adjectives/*
- *http://www.mml.cam.ac.uk/aspects/assets/abm33/places.htm*

Web Sites

WRITING

Varieties of Food

Given below are some popular fast food joints. Write a short note on the variety of food available at any one of the places:

McDonald's	Domino's Pizza	Orange Julius
Burger King	Pizza Hut	Subway Shoppe
Kentucky Fried Chicken	Godfather's Pizza	

LANGUAGE FOCUS

Presentation

Make a presentation on the view of your city from the top floor of your hotel.

Idioms and Expressions Related to Food

We know that 'to be in a soup' means to be in trouble. Similarly, 'to be in a jam' and 'to be in a pickle' indicate being in a difficult situation. Let's consider some more food-related expressions:

i. **As American as apple pie:** Something or somebody typically American.
ii. **Butterfingers:** A person who often drops things.
iii. **Butter wouldn't melt in his/her mouth:** Said of someone who seems to be innocent and good when he is not really so.
iv. **To wake up and smell the coffee:** To become aware of what is really happening in a situation, especially when this is something unpleasant.
v. **A tough cookie:** A smart and tough person.
vi. **To have your cake and eat it too:** To have both things that are available, to take advantage of everything.
vii. **A piece of the pie (British: a slice of the cake):** A share of the benefits.
viii. **Take the cake:** To do the most annoying and stupid things.
ix. **Ham-handed (British: ham fisted):** Lacking skills when using hands or dealing with people.
x. **To hold out an olive branch:** To offer a truce. The olive branch is a symbol of peace.
xi. **You can't make an omelette without breaking the egg:** You cannot achieve important results without minor setbacks.
xii. **To have egg all over your face:** To be made to look stupid.
xiii. **To put all your eggs in one basket:** To rely on one particular course of action to achieve something.
xiv. **To get one's just desserts:** To get what one deserves.
xv. **Cakewalk:** Something extremely easy.
xvi. **Pie in the sky:** An event that is unlikely to happen.
xvii. **Chicken:** A coward. (Similarly, **to chicken out** is to decide not to do something because one is too scared to do it.)

xviii. **To turn to jelly:** To feel weak because of fright or nervousness
xix. **To bring home the bacon:** To earn money.
xx. **To save somebody's bacon:** To rescue someone from a difficult situation.
xxi. **The cream of something:** The best of something.
xxii. **To cream somebody off:** To take away someone's best possession
xxiii. **Hot dog:** A person who performs clever and dangerous tricks while surfing or skiing.
xxiv. **Hot potato:** A difficult problem to deal with.
xxv. **Couch potato:** A person who spends a lot of time watching television.
xxvi. **Meat and potatoes:** Dealing with the important aspects of something.
xxvii. **No spring chicken:** No longer young

Exercise 1

Fill in the blanks using appropriate idioms from the above list:

i. She cleared her exams easily; it was almost a ____________ for her.
ii. You should dress your age; after all you're no ____________.
iii The kitchen staff keep breaking things; they are all ____________.
iv. The arrogant boss was fired by the management; truly he got ____________.
v. You must apply at least three places; one must not ____________.
i. Although she acts as if ____________, she is quite clever.
ii. To pass this exam is not going to be a ____________.
iii. The principal could not tackle the situation well; he is generally quite ____________.
iv. Rohan has committed several mistakes before, but this one ____________.
v. Don't underestimate the manager, he is a ____________.

Exercise 2

Match the following

i.	No spring chicken	a.	You cannot achieve important results without minor setbacks
ii.	To hold out an olive branch	b.	Something extremely easy
iii.	Cakewalk	c.	A symbol of peace
iv.	You can't make an omelette without breaking the egg	d.	No longer young
v.	To put all your eggs in one basket	e.	The best of something
vi.	To bring home the bacon	f.	A difficult problem to deal with
vii.	The cream of something	g.	To rely on one particular course of action to achieve something
viii.	Hot potato	h.	To earn money

REAL-LIFE READS

Hotel Regency

Pre-reading Activity

Which is the most popular restaurant in your hotel or in a hotel in your city? What are those features that make the place so successful? Discuss in groups.

Reading

Now read the following advertisement and answer the questions that follow:

Advertisements

The Regency

Hyderabad, India

A Business Hotel

A business class hotel conveniently located in the heart of Nizam's city. The hotel is within walking distance from the railway station and is easily accessible from Hyderabad International Airport.

The hotel offers 70 rooms and 8 well-appointed suites, centrally air-conditioned, with satellite TV, direct dial telephone with STD/ISD and wi-fi connectivity in all rooms.

Tariff

Room Type	Single	Double
Deluxe Room	7,500	15,000
Executive Club	6,500	13,000
Executive Premier	6,000	12,000
Suite		10,000
King's Suite		18,000
Extra Person: 1,000 + Tax		

1.25 per cent luxury tax will be applicable on room tariff.
5.15 per cent service tax will be applicable on room tariff.
12.5 per cent VAT will be applicable on food and beverages.

The above-mentioned rates are subject to change with/without prior notice.

Checkout: 12 noon

Restaurants

Bahaar

This multi-cuisine restaurant is a gourmet's delight, serving authentic Indian, Chinese, Continental, Thai and Hyderabadi Cuisine.
Daily lunch buffet from 12 noon to 3 pm.
Live Western music from 7.30 pm to 0.30 pm.

Ah, Milano

Serving authentic Italian cuisine.

Resto

A chic lounge bar with Mediterranean style décor, famed for its superb cocktails ambience.

Lime Tree

The trendiest coffee shop in town; with an array of melt-in-the-mount pastries and a selection of breads and snacks.

Conference and Banquets

Well-equipped conference halls accommodating up to 25 to 300 persons.

Business Centre

The Duke's Desk has business chamber with secretarial services, fax, Internet services and a board-room for executive meetings.

Wellness

Well-equipped fitness centre.

Services

Twenty-hour-hour room service, laundry, doctor-on-call, currency exchanged, travel desk.
All major credit cards accepted.

Exercise 1

Match the following:

	VENUE		KIND OF SERVICE
i.	Resto	a.	Italian cuisine
ii.	Ah, Milano	b.	Hyderabadi cuisine
iii.	Lime Tree	c.	Cocktails
iv.	The Duke's Desk	d.	Coffee shop
v.	Bahaar	e.	Business

Exercise 2

Fill in the blanks using the words given in the box:

chic	snacks	authentic	accessible	executive

a. The airport is easily ____________ from the hotel.
b. The rooms of this hotel are quite ____________ and therefore the fare is very high.
c. On the way to the theatre, we bought some ____________ from the restaurant round the corner.
d. This place is known for its ____________ Chinese food.
e. The members needed refreshments once the ____________ meeting got over.

APPRECIATING LITERATURE

Pre-reading Activity

Very often speakers/writers use adjectives to describe objects in order to add colour and variety to their language. Use suitable adjectives for the following nouns:

- Street
- Market
- Fountain
- Car

Reading

Read the following excerpt from E.M. Forster's novel.

A Room with a View

By *E.M. Forster*

It was pleasant to wake up in Florence, to open the eyes upon a bright bare room, with a floor of red tiles which look clean though they are not; with a painted ceiling whereon pink griffins and blue amorini sport in a forest of yellow violins and bassoons. It was pleasant, too, to fling wide the windows, pinching the fingers in unfamiliar fastenings, to lean out into sunshine with beautiful hills and trees and marble churches opposite, and close below, the Arno, gurgling against the embankment of the road.

Over the river men were at work with spades and sieves on the sandy foreshore, and on the river was a boat, also diligently employed for some mysterious end. An electric tram came rushing underneath the window. No one was inside it, except one tourist; but its platforms were overflowing with Italians, who preferred to stand. Children tried to hang on behind, and the conductor, with no malice, spat in their faces to make them let go. Then soldiers appeared—good-looking, undersized men—wearing each a knapsack covered with mangy fur, and a greatcoat which had been cut for some larger soldier. Beside them walked officers, looking foolish and fierce, and before them went little boys, turning somersaults in time with the band. The tramcar became entangled in their ranks, and moved on painfully, like a caterpillar in a swarm of ants. One of the little boys fell down, and some white bullocks came out of an archway. Indeed, if it had not been for the good advice of an old man who was selling button-hooks, the road might never have got clear.

Over such trivialities as these many a valuable hour may slip away, and the traveller who has gone to Italy to study the tactile values of Giotto, or the corruption of the Papacy, may return remembering nothing but the blue sky and the men and women who live under it. So it was as well that Miss Bartlett should tap and come in, and having commented on Lucy's leaving the door unlocked, and on her leaning out of the window before she was fully dressed, should urge her to hasten herself, or the best of the day would be gone. By the time Lucy was ready her cousin had done her breakfast, and was listening to the clever lady among the crumbs.

They drifted through a series of those grey-brown streets, neither commodious nor picturesque, in which the eastern quarter of the city abounds. Lucy soon lost interest in the discontent of

Lady Louisa, and became discontented herself. For one ravishing moment Italy appeared. She stood in the Square of the Annunziata and saw in the living terracotta those divine babies whom no cheap reproduction can ever stale. There they stood, with their shining limbs bursting from the garments of charity, and their strong white arms extended against circlets of heaven. Lucy thought she had never seen anything more beautiful; but Miss Lavish, with a shriek of dismay, dragged her forward, declaring that they were out of their path now by at least a mile.

The hour was approaching at which the continental breakfast begins, or rather ceases, to tell, and the ladies bought some hot chestnut paste out of a little shop, because it looked so typical. It tasted partly of the paper in which it was wrapped, partly of hair oil, partly of the great unknown. But it gave them strength to drift into another Piazza, large and dusty, on the farther side of which, rose a black-and-white facade of surpassing ugliness. Miss Lavish spoke to it dramatically. It was Santa Croce. The adventure was over.

Exercise 1

i. Name the three characters mentioned in the passage.
ii. What is the writer's opinion on the Italian people?
iii. Mention any two landmarks of Italy mentioned in the passage.

Exercise 2

In the first paragraph of the passage, you saw how the writer uses adjectives to describe objects. Is there a difference between the way you described the words given in the pre-reading exercise, and the author's use of adjectives?

Now use suitable adjectives for the following nouns:

- Room
- Corridor
- Restaurant
- Garden
- Spa
- Lobby
- Dining hall

PRONUNCIATION PRACTICE

Places in the Hotel

Practise pronouncing the following words:

Basement	China cabinet	Sewer grate	Pantry
French windows	Trash lorry	White noise	Patio
Hedge clipping	Lounge	Utility room	Cellar
Sideboard	Laundry hamper	Landing	Loft

13

Booking a Taxi

Situation

- Renting a car
- Booking air travel

Real-life Reads

- Prose passages
- Spa pamphlet

Grammar Bin

- The simple future tense (shall/will)

Speaking

- Upgrading a customer's request

Pronunciation Practice

- Everyday words

SITUATION

Renting a Car

Travellers often rent cars to commute within the city they are visiting. Read and practise the following conversation.

Joy: Hi, I'm Joy Gupta. I spoke to you over the phone this morning about renting a car.
Agent: Of course, Mr Gupta. Please take a seat and tell me your requirements.
Joy: Well, I'm planning a road trip to Ooty, shortly, with my family. We are three people. I need an *economy* car *Friday through Sunday*.
Agent: Do you have a driving licence?
Joy: Yes, I have an American *driver's license,* along with an Indian and an international one. Is that all right?
Agent: Yes, I believe so. May I have a look at them, please?
Joy: Sure. Here they are.
Agent: They seem perfectly valid. I don't think there would be any difficulty in your renting a car. Would you mind waiting while I check your driving records?
Joy: Not at all. Please take your time.
(The agent checks the papers).
Agent: Your record looks just fine. However, you would have to sign a contract attesting that you were never involved in a drunk driving offence. It's just a formality, Mr Gupta. We expect all our clients to sign such a contract.
Joy: Would you need any more documents?
Agent: Yes. We would also require a valid *credit card.*
Joy: All right. But I was thinking of making a cash payment.
Agent: That's perfectly fine, but a credit card is needed regardless of the mode of payment.
Joy: Will a *debit card* do? It's a Master Card.
Agent: I'm sorry, we don't accept debit cards. Could I see a *bona fide* credit card, please?
Joy: Absolutely. Here you are.
Agent: Thank you. All your documents look good. So, on what dates would you need the car?
Joy: Actually, this *very* weekend. Would it be possible?
Agent: This weekend is the second through fourth. Yes, it could work out well, I suppose. We can get you a *sedan,* which would be ideal for a family of three.
Joy: Fine. And since it's not *peak* time, can I hope to get a discount?
Agent: Sure. I guess we could give you an off-peak discount of around 10 per cent.
Joy: Thanks, that'd be really nice. Could you tell me about other deals and *specials*?
Agent: Have you rented a car with our company before? We have special discounts with our regular clients, and also special services at certain *motel*s on the way.
Joy: I'm afraid this is my first dealing with your company, so that *counts me out* for these privileges. But hang on! I am a member of the *frequent rental programme.* Here, this is my membership number.
Agent: Great. I think that'll fetch you a 5 per cent discount. Do you have a *frequent flier programme* number? We consider that, too, for certain special benefits.

Joy: No, it's a pity that I never took a membership of the frequent flier programme. Never mind. But I think my credit card covers me for loss damage, collision damage, physical damage and loss of personal effects. Isn't it?
Agent: Yes, I believe so. Would you like us to send the car to your residence or would you *pick it up* yourself?
Joy: I'd like to pick it as well as drop it off at your office. Do you have discounts for this?
Agent: As a matter of fact, yes. We'd offer you a 5 per cent location discount for that. You see, when a client picks up and drops the car, he's essentially doing us a favour.
Joy: Good. Then I'll be here on the second, 6 am sharp. And that reminds me, do you offer CD-ROMs that *map out the route*?
Agent: I'm afraid we do not offer that service. But I can suggest to you some shops that sell such CDs. Here, take a look at this brochure, it enlists all the major travel bookstores of the city.
Joy: Thank you, you have been extremely helpful.
Agent: Thank you Mr Gupta for doing business with us. We shall look forward to seeing you again. Have a nice day.

Idioms and Expressions Related to Car Rentals

i. **Rental car policy:** Policy that car rental agencies follow.
ii. **Driver's licence:** (British/Indian English driving licence): A document that certifies someone's driving capacity.
iii. **Limited coverage:** Insurance coverage where amount paid back will be limited (and not full).
iv. **Peak time:** (here) Time when the traffic is maximum.
v. **Motel:** A small hotel with boarding, lodging and car parking facility.
vi. **Frequent flier programme:** Points and rewards provided by airlines to those passengers who fly regularly with them.
vii. **Personal effects:** Articles of personal use, items owned by a person.
viii. **Bona fide:** Authentic.
ix. **Economy:** Budget.

Exercise 1

Fill in the blanks using the above words:

i. We must start for the airport early; there may be a traffic jam during the ____________.
ii. It's a long drive, we must stop at a ____________ on the way.
iii. They've accumulated plenty of points through the ____________.
iv. Do carry your ____________, the traffic police may ask you to produce one.
v. They're flying ____________ class because the business class is very expensive.

Booking Air Travel

People often book air tickets through travel agents. Read and practise the following conversation.

Ajit: Hi. I'd like to *book* a flight from Chennai to Paris.
Travel Agent: Certainly. When would you like to go?
Ajit: Three weeks from now. But tell me, how much would it cost?
Travel Agent: It would cost you about ₹80,000, for a round trip.
Ajit: And how much time in advance should I book to get a discount?
Travel Agent: Well, ideally speaking, a month in advance.
Ajit: Alright, then please book a ticket for me one month from today.
Travel Agent: Will it be a one-way or round trip?
Ajit: It would be a round trip.
Travel Agent: May I have your name and address, please?
Ajit: Sure. The name's Ajit Bansal, that's A-J-I-T B-A-N-S-A-L. And the address is 12, T. Nagar.
Travel Agent: Do you have insurance? Or shall we arrange one for you?
Ajit: Thank you. I'm insured all right. I've a trip cancellation as well as a medical assistance insurance.
Travel Agent: Do you have any particular airline on mind?
Ajit: Well, I've always preferred United Airlines. In fact, I'm a frequent flier with them.
Travel Agent: Great. Would you like to take business class?
Ajit: No, I'd rather take the coach.
Travel Agent: Very well. Would it be smoking or non-smoking?
Ajit: Non-smoking, please.
Travel Agent: Fine (*Types in the details*). You are booked on flight number 503. Departure time 6:30 am and arrival time 7:35 am next morning. Would you like to buy a ticket now?
Ajit: I don't really think so. I'll get it at the airport.
Travel Agent: All right, sir. You are all confirmed to fly on the 12th next month.
Ajit: Thank you.
Travel Agent: You're welcome, and have a nice day.

REAL-LIFE READS

Pre-reading Activity
Describe the travel desk in your hotel to your class. Your talk must include the following:

- What does the place look like?
- Who are the people who work there?
- What happens there?

Reading
Read the following passage and answer the questions that follow:

Cars for Hire

Cars Rental India is a professional rental firm with cheap and convenient rental services available across India. Covering all the major cities like Delhi, Mumbai, Kolkata and Goa, Cars Rental India has excellent car hire deals and a variety of pick up destinations, spread throughout this country.

India: Land of Festivals

India is a multicultural country with a long history to it. The seventh largest country in the world, India is known for its ethnicity, culture and cuisine. From metropolitan cities to small towns, India has plenty to offer in terms of sightseeing. Located in the northern part of this country, its capital city, Delhi is thousand years old and has played a major role in its history. Ruled by the *Moghuls* for centuries, Delhi has many old monuments and buildings, such as Red Fort, Humayun's Tomb, Qutub Minar and many more. India Gate is a major war monument built in memory of martyrs of First World War. The Jama Masjid and the Akshardham Temple are some popular religious sites located in the capital. Mumbai is another important Indian city known as the financial capital of the country.

The home to Indian cinema, or 'Bollywood', Mumbai is also famous for attractions like Aksa beach, Marine Drive, Chowpati and Haji Ali. Other major notable Indian cities that are worth visiting are Varanasi, Goa, Shimla, Kochi and Bangalore.

Being a country with diverse cultures and religions, India has many interesting things to see and attractions like the Golden Temple, the Taj Mahal, the Lake Palace, the Ajanta and Ellora caves and the Khajuraho temples top the list of outstanding landmarks in India. Delhi and Mumbai are hubs for many business travellers arriving in this country. India also hosts numerous religious and cultural festivals throughout the year. Get yourself an affordable car on rent from Cars Rental India to get familiar with India's culture, cuisine and attractions.

Our services include:

- Collision damage waiver (CDW)
- Vehicle theft waiver
- Liability insurance
- Premium location/ airport fee
- VAT local tax
- Road fund tax (RFT)
- Unlimited mileage
- 24 hours road assistance

(Adapted from 'Welcome to Cars Rental India' from *http://www.carsrentalindia.net/*).

Dictionary Work

Using a dictionary, find the meanings of the following terms:

- Collision damage waiver (CDW): ____________________
- Vehicle theft waiver: ____________________
- Liability insurance: ____________________
- Premium location/airport fee: ____________________
- VAT local tax: ____________________
- Road fund tax (RFT): ____________________
- Unlimited mileage 24 hours road assistance: ____________________

On the Road

Work in pairs and give another term for the following, choosing from the box below:

Emergency brake	Minivan	Parking lot	High-octane
Trunk hood	Turn signals	Muffler	Fender

i. Another name for premium gasoline. ____________________
ii. A device which is required in a car to prevent it from making noise. ____________________
iii. Bonnet. ____________________
iv. This can be attached to your car for loading heavy stuff. ____________________
v. You park your car here. ____________________
vi. Windscreen wiper. ____________________
vii. Handbrake. ____________________
viii. Indicators. ____________________
ix. Boot. ____________________

Exercise 1

Complete the details in the following form of a car rental agency:

Car Rental Form

Name: ____________________

Car required: ____________________ Make: ____________________

Kind of insurance required:

Full: ____________________ Partial: ____________________

From

- Time:
- Day:
- Month:
- Year:

To

- Time:
- Day:
- Month:
- Year:

Pick-up location: ______________________________

Return location: ______________________________

Know the Driving Terms

Discuss the following questions in pairs. Share your answers with the rest of the class:

i. Do you have to pay toll while driving on major highways?
ii. How old should you be to rent a car?
iii. What licence do you need to rent a car?
iv. What is a divided highway?
v. What is a driver's manual?
vi. What is a child safety seat?
vii. What is a compact car?
viii. What is a luxury car?
ix. What can happen if you drink and drive?
x. What do you do on seeing a yellow traffic light?
xi. What is a car upgrade?

Visiting a Spa

Pre-reading Activity

Highlight the main features of the spa or the health care centre of your hotel or any hotel you know.

Reading

Now read the following passage and answer the questions that follow:

Pamphlets

Rejuvenate Your Body at Caretake

The complete health and beauty centre at The Regency, Caretake

- rejuvenates
- relaxes
- refreshes

CareMaya

This Ayurvedic centre offers a complete programme to recoup your energy with Ayurvedic massage, herbal rejuvenation therapies and yoga therapy. Therapies are carried out under the specialized care of our experts. At the end of a hectic day of activities we help you unwind and refresh.

Marmakizhi Therapy

This is a combination of massage and rejuvenation therapy. It is a very relaxing yet stimulating experience, invigorating and leading to a wonderful sense of calmness and well-being. It is a safe treatment for back pain, joint pain, sprains, nervous weakness, rheumatism, etc. For this treatment, we make a mixture of different herbal powders and tie it in a cloth bag. After the massage, this bag is heated in medicated oil and administered on the body.

Steambath

In this therapy, the person is made to perspire inside a steam chamber. It helps to tone the skin, open pores and removes toxins from the body.

Njavara Therapy

It strengthens the weak muscles, improves blood and lymphatic circulation and makes you feel young. It treats chronic physical problems like back pain, slip disc, spondilities, sciatica, rheumatism, etc. Njavara is a preparation of a special type of rice boiled in the essence or medicinal herbs and milk and wrapped in a cloth bag. After the massage, this herbal bag is dipped in the mixture of hot milk and essence of medicinal herbs and administered on the entire body.

Pizhichil

This is a herbal fomentation therapy combined with sukha massage. This treatment is best for holistic healing, rejuvenation of body and mind. Pizhichil means squeezing of a cloth soaked in oil over the body. This therapy is good for severe type of rheumatism, paralysis, nervous weakness, etc.

Raksha Rejuvenation

With age, various cells and tissues of the body undergo changes, so it is necessary to rejuvenate the body systems for better harmony of the body, mind and soul. To maintain health, youth and beauty of the body and to eliminate toxins, the Raksha rejuvenation package is very effective. It includes yoga therapy.

Exercise 1

i. What are the benefits of a steambath?

____

____

ii. Njavra therapy involves ______________________________

____

iii. Pizhichil means ______________________________

____

Exercise 2

Match the following:

SL. NO.	THERAPY	SL. NO.	RESULT
a.	Marmakizhi therapy	i.	Improves blood and lymphatic circulation
b.	Raksha	ii.	Holistic healing
c.	Njavara therapy	iii.	Back pain and rheumatism
d.	Pizhichil	iv.	Eliminates toxins

Exercise 3

Write down the opposites of the following words using 'un' or 'in':

i. Effective: ____________________

ii. Specialized: ____________________

iii. Necessary: ____________________

iv. Safe: ____________________

v. Stimulating: ____________________

GRAMMAR BIN

The Simple Future Tense (shall/will)

The simple future tense is formed by *shall/will* for the first person singular or plural and *will* for the second and third persons (singular or plural) + the infinitive (without to).

Will

We often use *will* as a neutral way of expressing the future, and it is the most common way of expressing this tense. For example, *I will be going to Shimla this summer*. We use *will* for an instant decision, when we decide on something or agree to do it more or less at the moment of speaking. Look at the following sentences:

- I am hungry. I *will* boil some vegetables.
- *I'll* pay you back soon.

The contracted form of *will* is (I/you/we/they)*'ll* and *won't* (for indicting negative) which is permitted in spoken English but rarely used in formal and academic contexts. We can also make use of *will* for a prediction about the future. For example, 'People will travel to Mars someday.'

Shall

Nowadays *shall* is rarely used, except in the Interrogative, where it is always used for the first person. For example, *Shall we go? I shall know the results soon.*

Shall is a little formal compared to *will.*

Exercise 1

Make sentences using the words given. The first sentence has been done for you as an example:

i. it/be/rain/today…It will rain today
ii. Rohan/watch/the match/night
iii. Neel/be/happy on hearing this news
iv. Harry/be/not pass
v. I/be/careful
vi. The festival/be/fun

Learn more about using the future tense from the following web sites:

- *http://www.englishpage.com/verbpage/simplefuture.html*
- *http://www.englishclub.com/grammar/verb-tenses_future.htm*

Web Sites

Exercise 2

Fill in the blanks with the appropriate form of verbs in the future tense given in brackets:

i. If you are ready, we _______________ (start) for the airport.
ii. If we don't start now, we _______________ (miss) the flight.
iii. Don't stand in the hot sun, or else _______________ (get) fever.
iv. Call me after 9 pm, we _______________ (discuss) this in detail.
v. If the hotel does not improve its services soon, clients _______________ (stop) coming here.

SPEAKING

Upgrading a Customer's Request

Discussion

Imagine that Joy Gupta arrives at a car rental office on the morning of 2 March, at 5.30 am to pick up his sedan. A sedan is an economy class vehicle, of which the office is facing a shortage. They offer to upgrade Joy to a higher car class. Act out the dialogue between the agent and Joy.

PRONUNCIATION PRACTICE

Everyday Words

Pronounce the following words:

Brochure	Contract	Cancellation
Collision	Sedan	Insurance
Record		

14

Taking a Message

Situation
- Taking a message
- Communicating a message

Vocabulary
- Word formation
- Telephone words
- More phrasal verbs

Speaking
- Service apartments

Pronunciation Practice
- More numbers

Appreciating Literature
- *Dusk*, by Saki

SITUATION

Taking a Message

Discussion
How do you take and convey messages in your job?

You will be required to take messages for guests staying in your hotel. Read and practise the following conversation about a guest who needs to be given a message.

Receptionist: Hotel Sunrise, good afternoon.
Caller: Hi, could you connect me to room 304, please? That's Mrs Abraham's room. I'm Savita, her colleague from Chandigarh.
Receptionist: I'm sorry, Mrs Abraham just left for the conference.
Caller: Oh, any idea when she would be back?
Receptionist: I'm afraid I don't have the exact time, but usually she returns by 6 in the evening.
Caller: Can I leave a message with you?
Receptionist: Certainly, madam.
Caller: Please tell her that her parcel of books from Amazon.com has just arrived. She has been expecting them for quite a while.
Receptionist: I've taken down the message, madam. I'll make sure that she gets it. Is there anything you would like to add?
Caller: Yes, please take down my mobile number, in case she decides to call me back. It is 9444388000.
Receptionist: Thank you, madam. We'll deliver the message as soon as she returns.

Communicating a Message

You should be able to deliver messages for your guests correctly. Read and practise the following conversation.

Staff: Good evening, madam. How was your day?
Guest: Good, but very tiring.
Staff: Here's your room key, madam.
Guest: Thank you so much.
Staff: And madam, there was a message from your colleague from Chandigarh.
Guest: I see, what is it?
Staff: Here's the note, madam.
Guest: Thank you.
Staff: You're welcome, madam.

Exercise 1

Take a message from a caller for a guest in your hotel. Write it down in the following format:

Telephone Message

For ____________________

Room number ____________________

From ____________________

Time ____________________

Message ____________________

____

____

Exercise 2

Match the situations with the appropriate responses:

SL. NO.	SITUATION	SL. NO.	RESPONSE
i.	Can I speak to Mr Krishnan in room 34?	a.	Can I take a message, sir?
ii.	I've been trying to contact Mr Krishnan in room 34 but no one's responding.	b.	I'm afraid the line is busy at the moment. Would you like to call back after sometime?
iii.	Could you connect me to room 34, please?	c.	Room 34, madam? I'll put you through.

Exercise 3

Complete the following dialogues by filling in the blanks:

i. **Staff:** Good afternoon, Grand Hotel, ___________ I help you?
Caller: Yes, can you ___________ me to Jenny Richards in ___________?
Staff: I'm sorry the ___________ is busy, would you like ___________
Caller: Not really, I would like to ___________ a message.

ii. **Staff:** Hello, could you ___________ me to room 854, please?
Caller: ___________, there's no one there. Would you like to leave ___________
Staff: ____________________________________

VOCABULARY

Word Formation

Exercise 1

Split the following words till you get the root word. For example, *unforgiven* can be analyzed as un+forgive+en, where the root word is forgive.

i. Hostility
ii. Emptiness
iii. Appearance
iv. Irresolutely
v. Carelessness

Telephone Words

You will encounter the following words while taking and delivering messages.

- **Answer call:** A telephone service that lets us get messages when we do not answer.
- **Area code:** Indian English: STD code. The three-digit code for the region where one lives. For example, 011 for New Delhi and 212 for New York City.
- **Call forwarding:** A service that enables us to send your calls to another number.
- **Call-in** (British English: phone–in): A programme on television or radio that helps people to make telephone calls and ask questions or make comments.
- **Call waiting:** A service that helps us to switch to another caller while we are on the phone with someone.
- **Collect:** A long-distance call that reverses the charges. The person who we call pays the bill.
- **Flat rate:** A fixed rate, regardless of the number of local calls we make.
- **Information:** Indian English: 197. This is the number we dial to get somebody's telephone number.
- **Pay phone:** A public telephone, which works by using a card or a coin.
- **Person to person:** Here, we tell the operator the name of the person we want to talk to. If the person is not there, the operator does not put the call through.
- **Speakerphone:** A phone with which people can speak and hear without holding the receiver.
- **Switchboard:** The central part of a telephone system used by a company or office, where telephone calls are answered and connected to the appropriate person or department.
- **Toll-free:** Free calls.
- **Three-way calling:** A service that lets us talk to three people on three separate lines at the same time.
- **White pages:** A book that helps us find the telephone numbers of homes, businesses and government offices.
- **Yellow pages:** A telephone directory for the numbers of stores and services.

Exercise 2

Fill in the blanks with the words given below:

Dial tone	White pages	Extension	Pager	Redial	Forward the call
Answer call	Flat rate	Call in	Information	Call back	

i. I think the phone is not working, there is no ___________.

ii. This ___________ is a blessing. Otherwise, my teenage sister would have forced me to pay a huge bill.

iii. I think this is not the right ___________. Could you put me on the switchboard, please?

iv. Do you know that Ronaldo will be on CNN tomorrow for the ___________ show?

v. We don't have Tom's number. Shall we ask the ___________?

More Phrasal Verbs

You have already learned something about phrasal verbs in the previous chapter. Here is a list which will help you know more.

Table 14.1 Phrasal Verbs

SL. NO.	PHRASAL VERB	MEANING	EXAMPLE
i.	Do something to someone/thing	Cause something to happen	What have you done to yourself?
ii.	Do with something	Be concerned with	He had something to do with the founding of the student's paper at Johns Hopkins University.
iii.	Do without someone	Manage without	We are doing without a dietician since the last one left.
iv.	Fit in with someone/something	Work with	She would not be able to fit in with our hospital system.
v.	Get at someone	Criticize someone	The matron is always trying to get at the trainees.
vi.	Do someone in	Exhaust	At the end of the shift, I feel completely done in.
vii.	Get on	Progress	Take this treatment for a month and let's see how you get on.
viii.	Go under	Have an anaesthetic	The patient went under at 11 and came around at 2 o'clock.
ix.	Keep someone from doing something	Prevent	My cough keeps me from sleeping.
x.	Keep to something	Adhere to	You must keep to this diet till your throat gets better.
xi.	Let someone down	Disappoint	I cannot let the doctor down and will do this extra shift.
xii.	Let up	Become less intense	I wish this pain would let up for a while.
xiii.	Look after someone	Take care of	Who looks after the child when you come on duty?

SL. NO.	PHRASAL VERB	MEANING	EXAMPLE
xiv.	Look on	Watch something without taking part	The interns looked on as the surgeon performed the operation.
xv.	Look through something	Examine papers	The doctor looked through the nurses' notes.
xvi.	Look someone/ something up	Visit someone/search for a word/fact	If you don't know the meaning of the word, look it up in the dictionary.
xvii.	Make someone out	Understand someone's behaviour	I can't make her out at all.
xviii.	Put someone away	To confine someone to prison/a psychiatric unit	The old man has been put away by his family.
xix.	Run across someone	To meet someone by chance	She has never run across this man before.
xx.	Take on something	Agree to work	She has taken on too much work and cannot complete anything according to schedule.

Exercise 1

Fill in the blanks using phrasal verbs from the above list.

i. The judge ordered the murderer to be ____________ for 20 years.
ii. Facebook has made it easy for people to ____________ their friends.
iii. The trainees ____________ as the master chef cooked a dish.
iv. He can ____________ his assistant's help.
v. It is difficult to ____________ George, since he is so moody.

Exercise 2

Use the following phrasal verbs in sentences of your own. You can use the dictionary to find their meanings:

- Break out: ____

  ____
- Break down: ____

  ____
- Break through: ____

  ____
- Break up: ____

  ____
- Come about: ____

  ____

- Come over: ____

____

- Come across: ____

____

- Come through: ____

____

- Cut someone off: ____

____

- Get about: ____

____

- Get over something: ____

____

SPEAKING

Service Apartments

Collect information about service apartments in your town or city. Discuss the advantages and disadvantages of living in them.

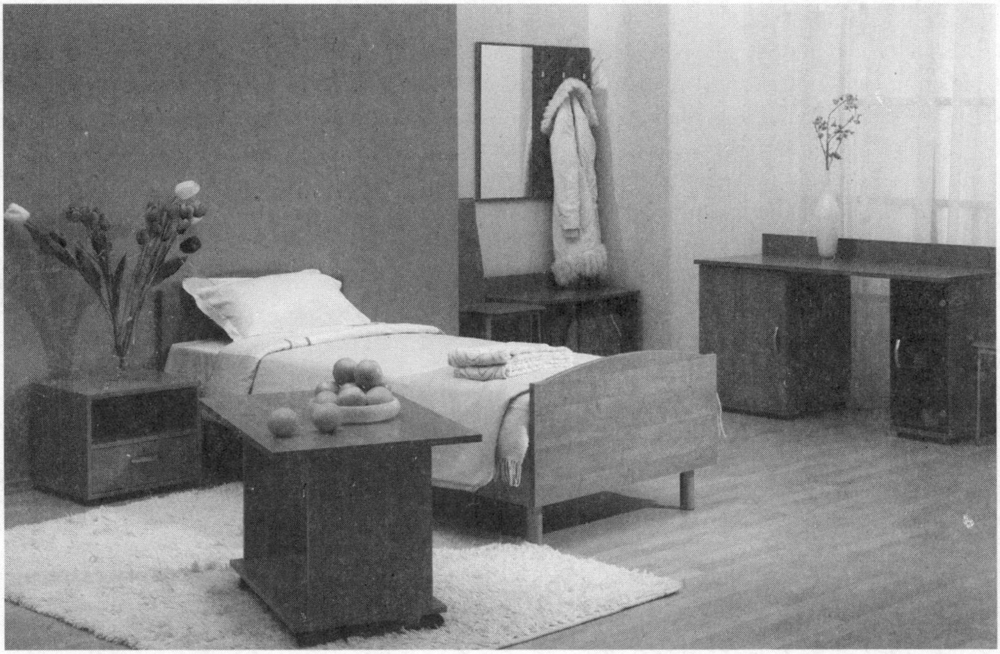

Exercise 1
Fill in the blanks using words given in the box below:

amenities	obviates	relocating	adaptation process
impersonal	cramp	leisure	group coordination

Service Apartments

For many travellers, staying in a service apartment is the first option when they travel for a longer period. There is more than one reason why you should choose a service apartment over a hotel for your business and ________ travels. Service apartments, also known as a part hotels, corporate housing and extended stay hotels offer travellers somewhere to live rather than just a place to stay. Hotels are, for the most part, ________ in feel but a serviced apartment gives such a feeling like staying at home.

A hotel room can ________ your style but a service apartment lets you entertain the way you want to. It's just like having your own space and it makes meetings, events and having family over easier (especially if you are ________) with separate spaces for living, sleeping, eating, cooking and working.

A service apartment is a perfect choice for visitors who are relocating, working on a contract, executives on a short visit or colleagues travelling together. Avoid the 'hotel feel' and enjoy ________ such as broadband, flat panel TV, digital or cable channels and a fully fitted kitchen at an all-inclusive price, and make your business trip an exceptional stay. Service apartment rates are per apartment and not per person so there can be significant money savings especially when you travel with the family or in big group. It usually has a fully equipped kitchen which ________ the need to eat out all the time.

Besides saving money, a service apartment can reduce the hassle of ________ when you travel in big group or with the family. You can book a 3-bedroom apartment and you will get private bedrooms for each member of the family plus a living and dining area for the whole family.

Staying in a service apartment can be a huge benefit during relocation. The first few weeks or months in a new country can be difficult and disorienting. A service apartment with the space and amenities of home helps to smooth that adaptation process. With the above good reasons and the growing popularity of serviced apartments, why don't you opt for a service apartment on your next trip?

PRONUNCIATION PRACTICE

More Numbers

Practise the pronunciation of the following numbers:

044-2345 4568	08654322239
011-4532 9990	95564 89447
022-9865 9866	0531 3213 0965
020 9955 3434	099-2255 2203

APPRECIATING LITERATURE

Pre-reading Activity

Describe a place of interest around your hotel. You must be able to talk about:

- What do people do there
- What kind of people come there
- When do people come to that place

Discussion

Discuss some more stories with a surprise ending. Share your stories with your group.

Reading

Read the following short story and answer the questions based on it:

Dusk

By *Saki*

Norman Gortsby sat on a bench in the Park. Hyde Park Corner, with its rattle and hoot of traffic, lay immediately to his right. It was some thirty minutes past six on an early March evening, and dusk had fallen heavily over the scene, dusk mitigated by some faint moonlight and many street lamps. There was a wide emptiness over road and sidewalk, and yet there were many figures moving silently through the half-light, or dotted on bench and chair, scarcely to be distinguished from the shadowed gloom in which they sat.

On the bench by his side sat an elderly gentleman. His clothes could scarcely be called shabby, at least they passed muster in the half-light, but one's imagination could not have pictured the wearer embarking on the purchase of a half-crown box of chocolates or laying out nine pence on a carnation buttonhole. As he rose to go Gortsby imagined him returning to a home circle where he was snubbed and of no account, or to some bleak lodging where his ability to pay a weekly bill was the beginning and end of the interest he inspired. His retreating figure vanished slowly into the shadows, and his place on the bench was taken almost immediately by a young man, fairly well dressed but scarcely more cheerful of mien than his predecessor. 'You don't seem in a very good temper,' said Gortsby.

The young man turned to him with a look of disarming frankness which put him instantly on his guard.

'You wouldn't be in a good temper if you were in the fix I'm in,' he said; 'I've done the silliest thing I've ever done in my life.'

'Yes?' said Gortsby.

'Came up this afternoon, meaning to stay at the Patagonian Hotel in Berkshire Square,' continued the young man; 'when I got there I found it had been pulled down some weeks ago and a cinema theatre run up on the site. The taxi driver recommended me to another hotel some way off and I went there. I just sent a letter to my people, giving them the address, and then I went out to buy some soap—I'd forgotten to pack any and I hate using hotel soap. Then I strolled about a bit, had a drink at a bar and looked at the shops, and when I came to turn my steps back to the hotel I suddenly realised that I didn't remember its name or even what street it was in. There's a nice predicament for a fellow who hasn't any friends or connections in London! Of course I can wire to my people for the address, but they won't have got my letter till tomorrow; meantime I'm without any money, came out with about a shilling on me, which went in buying the soap and getting the drink, and here I am, wandering about with two pence in my pocket and nowhere to go for the night.'

There was a pause after the story had been told, 'I suppose you think I've spun you rather an impossible yarn,' said the young man presently.

'Not at all impossible,' said Gortsby, 'I remember doing exactly the same thing once in a foreign capital, and on that occasion there were two of us, which made it more remarkable. Luckily we remembered that the hotel was on a sort of canal, and when we struck the canal we were able to find our way back to the hotel.'

The youth brightened at the reminiscence. 'In a foreign city I wouldn't mind so much,' he said; 'one could go to one's Consul and get the requisite help from him. Here in one's own land one is far more derelict if one gets into a fix. Unless I can find some decent chap to swallow my story and lend me some money I seem likely to spend the night on the Embankment. I'm glad, anyhow, that you don't think the story outrageously improbable.'

He threw a good deal of warmth into the last remark, as though perhaps to indicate his hope that Gortsby did not fall far short of the requisite decency.

'Of course,' said Gortsby slowly, 'the weak point of your story is that you can't produce the soap.'

The young man sat forward hurriedly, felt rapidly in the pockets of his overcoat, and then jumped to his feet.

'I must have lost it,' he muttered angrily.

'To lose an hotel and a cake of soap on one afternoon suggests wilful carelessness,' said Gortsby, but the young man scarcely waited to hear the end of the remark. He flitted away down the path, his head held high, with an air of somewhat jaded jauntiness.

'It was a pity,' mused Gortsby; 'the going out to get one's own soap was the one convincing touch in the whole story, and yet it was just that little detail that brought him to grief. If he had had the brilliant forethought to provide himself with a cake of soap, wrapped and sealed with all the solicitude of the chemist's counter, he would have been a genius in his particular line.'

With that reflection Gortsby rose to go; as he did so an exclamation of concern escaped him. Lying on the ground by the side of the bench was a small oval packet. It could be nothing else but a cake of soap, and it had evidently fallen out of the youth's overcoat pocket when he flung himself down on the seat. In another moment Gortsby was scudding along the dusk-shrouded path in anxious quest for a youthful figure in a light overcoat. He had nearly given up the search when he caught sight of the object of his pursuit standing irresolutely on the border of the carriage drive, evidently uncertain whether to strike across the Park or make for the bustling pavements of Knightsbridge. He turned round sharply with an air of defensive hostility when he found Gortsby hailing him.

'The important witness to the genuineness of your story has turned up,' said Gortsby, holding out the cake of soap; 'it must have slid out of your overcoat pocket when you sat down on the seat. I saw it on the ground after you left. You must excuse my disbelief, but appearances were really rather against you, and now, as I appealed to the testimony of the soap I think I ought to abide by its verdict. If the loan of a sovereign is any good to you'.

The young man hastily removed all doubt on the subject by pocketing the coin.

'Here is my card with my address,' continued Gortsby; 'any day this week will do for returning the money, and here is the soap—don't lose it again it's been a good friend to you.'

'Lucky thing your finding it,' said the youth, and then he blurted out a word or two of thanks and fled headlong in the direction of Knightsbridge.

'Poor boy, he as nearly as possible broke down,' said Gortsby to himself. 'I don't wonder either; the relief from his quandary must have been acute. It's a lesson to me not to be too clever in judging by circumstances.'

As Gortsby retraced his steps past the seat, he saw an elderly gentleman poking and peering beneath it and on all sides of it, and recognised his earlier fellow occupant.

'Have you lost anything, sir?' he asked.

'Yes, sir, a cake of soap.'

Hyde Park: *One of London's finest gardens, which has been frequently referred to in literature.*

Culture

Exercise 1

Answer the following questions.

i. Mention any three places in London referred to in the story.

____

____

____

ii. What did the elderly gentleman look like?

____

____

____

iii. What is the significance of the cake of soap in the story?

____

____

____

15

Checking Out

In This Unit

Situation
- Helping the guest with settling bills
- Seeing off guests

Vocabulary
- Food-related adjectives
- Synonyms

Real-life Reads
- Hôtel de la Place du Louvre

Grammar Bin
- Present perfect tense

Language Focus
- Making comparisons and contrasts
- Handling complaints and making suggestions
- Expressions of politeness

Workplace Skills
- Engaging audiences

Pronunciation Practice
- Workplace currencies

SITUATION

Helping the Guest with Settling Bills

When a guest leaves, the personnel manning the reception have to help him/ her to settle the bills. Read and practise the following conversation:

Guest: Hi, I am from room 509. I'm checking out this evening, please could you get my bills ready?
Staff: Sure, sir. Your bills are already ready. Here they are.
Guest: Could you explain these items on my bill, please?
Staff: Certainly, sir. Please tell me how I can help.
Guest: Did I really make three overseas calls?
Staff: Yes, sir. There are two calls to Paris and one to Manchester.
Guest: I see. And what is this 15 per cent charge here?
Staff: It's the service charge, sir.
Guest: Alright. Here's my credit card. You do accept American Express, don't you?
Staff: We do sir, thank you. Please be seated, I'll process the card in a moment.

Seeing Guests Off

Discussion
Explain a hotel bill to a guest who is checking out. Take turns in playing the two parts.

Guests leaving the hotel should be seen off politely. Read and practise the following conversation:

Guest: Are my bills all settled?
Staff: Yes, sir. Here's your credit card; and this is a copy of your bill.
Guest: Thank you. Is my cab ready?
Staff: It is, sir. The bellboy will take your luggage to the cab.
Guest: Oh great.
Staff: Goodbye, sir; have a nice trip. It was a pleasure having you with us.
Guest: Thank you. Goodbye.

VOCABULARY

Food-related Adjectives

Match the following:

i.	Wholesome	a.	Be careful about how many calories one has
ii.	Synthetic	b.	Be invited out to a restaurant
iii.	Count the calories	c.	Good for health, nutritious
iv.	To be wined and dined	d.	Artificial

Synonyms

Two words with the same meaning are called synonyms.

Exercise 1
Replace the italicized words with synonyms:

i. Please pull down the *blinds*, it's rather sunny.
ii. Polly has got to clean her *cupboard* today, it's in a complete mess.
iii. We need someone to help us with the *odd jobs* round the hotel.
iv. We need a plumber to fix this *faucet*.
v. I was shocked to hear that Remo got into a fight with the *bartender*.
vi. The bakery around the corner sells the best *cookies* in town.

REAL-LIFE READS

Hôtel de la Place du Louvre

Pre-reading Activity
Discuss the amenities available at your hotel. You should include the following topics:

- The swimming pool
- The health club/gym
- The beauty salon

Reading
Read the descriptions of some renowned hotels, and answer the questions that follow:

Pamphlets

a. Hôtel de la Place du Louvre, Paris

Combining Calm and a Central Location

Between the Pont Neuf and the Rue de Rivoli, the Hôtel de la Place du Louvre is located in a quiet street facing the Colonnade du Louvre and the Saint-Germain l'Auxerrois Church. It is an ideal base for visiting the George Pompidou Centre (Beaubourg), the Hôtel de Ville and the Marais district where you will enjoy the numerous shops and the splendid Place des Vosges.

In this characteristic old Parisian building, stonewalls and modern decor work wonderfully together. It is noticeable in the hall and the breakfast room which were both fully refurbished in contemporary and warm tones in 2009.

Breakfast is served in the 'Cave des Mousquetaires' (Musketeers), a cut stone vaulted cave that was once connected to the Louvre.

Each of the 20 rooms of the hotel is named after a famous painter. Some of them offer beautiful views of the Louvre. They are fitted with TRECA® beds, duvet and two types of pillows, a flat screen satellite television, free wi-fi access, mini-bar, telephone and air conditioning.

Hotel Services

- Continental breakfast served in the Cave des Mousquetaires or in your room (14€)
- Room service offered from 6 pm to 2 am
- Parking nearby
- Complimentary national and international newspapers
- Free Internet corner
- Airport transfer (extra cost—reservation required)
- English, Spanish, German and Luxembourgish spoken
- Check in starts at 2 pm. Check out by 12 pm.
- The front desk will be happy to assist you with any question related to your stay in Paris to make sure it is an unforgettable experience.

b. Four Seasons Hotels and Resorts

The story of Four Seasons Hotels and Resorts, which opened its first hotel in 1961, is a tale of continual innovation, remarkable expansion and single-minded dedication to the highest of standards. The Canada-based company has, for nearly 50 years, transformed the hospitality industry by combining friendliness and efficiency with the finest traditions of international hotel-keeping. In the process, Four Seasons has redefined luxury for the modern traveller.

Supremely comfortable, a room at Four Seasons begins with a liberating sense of space. Your guest room or suite is often among the destination's largest. Designed to inspire, its beauty connects you with the surrounding environment, while ensuring your comfort and convenience.

You'll enjoy a restful sleep because each sensory detail has been carefully refined to be just right. As have all the added touches, from the position of your high-speed network link to the precise depth of your soaking tub. You feel thoroughly at home, and completely at your best.

It offers superbly rewarding leisure time, with spa escapes, championship golf, active pursuits from skiing to scuba diving, cooking schools to fly fishing. Whether your vacation dream is action packed or more relaxed, the world of Four Seasons includes temptations for any interest, any season.

You are a heartbeat away from the things that inspire you in fascinating cities or sought-after resorts. From award-winning cuisine to the resourceful assistance of the multilingual concierge, being 'at leisure' at Four Seasons puts more on your fingertips.

c. The Hilton Singapore Hotel

This is our commitment to you: If you're not satisfied with your stay, let us know and we'll make it right.

Located on Orchard Road, Singapore's popular entertainment and shopping precinct, the Hilton Singapore Hotel is close to major shopping malls such as ION Orchard and Takashimaya Shopping Centre. Swim laps in the rooftop pool, work out in the fitness centre or relax with a massage at this central Singapore hotel. Located in the heart of Orchard Road, the hotel is just a 20-minute drive from the airport. Shop in the luxury boutiques of the two-storeyed shopping mall located within the hotel or for the more adventurous, go offsite for a night safari. Savour a meal at the il Cielo Italian Restaurant and Bar, spoil yourself with Sunday champagne brunch at Checkers Brasserie or enjoy the revitalizing organic juice in Glow Juice Bar and Café at the Hilton Singapore Hotel.

From Deluxe Rooms up, all Hilton Singapore's rooms have wireless Internet access and city views. Executive Rooms offer Executive Lounge access. Do business in 11 meeting rooms for 18 to 550 people and 2 business centres.

Guest Accommodations: Suite

Take in the vibrant view of Orchard Road from the floor-to-ceiling windows of this spacious, modern 53.7 sq. m/578 sq.ft suite offering a separate seating, working and dining area. Sit back and watch a DVD or surf the Web on a wireless Internet connection. Two bathrooms with granite features offer a separate bath tub and shower for rejuvenation. Enjoy access and full benefits of the Executive Lounge. Special extras include magazines, newspapers and fresh fruit.

Features and Highlights

- Executive rooms and executive lounge
- Rooftop pool with city views
- Fitness centre and two treatment rooms

Directions and Transportation: From Singapore Changi International Airport

- **Taxi:** Taxis are readily available to take you from the airport to the Hilton Singapore Hotel. The journey normally takes around 20 minutes from the airport to the hotel forecourt.
- **Train (MRT):** The train journey from the airport to Orchard MRT Station, the underground station nearest to Hilton Singapore hotel, normally takes around 40 minutes.

To get to the hotel from the underground station, walk through the underpass via ION Orchard shopping centre and proceed to the ground floor at the Orchard Road/ Paterson Road exit.

Hotel Policies

Check in: 2:00 pm; Check out: 12:00 pm

Parking: self-parking: SG$7 per hour; valet parking: SG$10. Add $SG7 per hour

Exercise 1

Answer the following questions:

i. Where is the Hôtel de la Place du Louvre situated?

____

____

____

ii. Where is the il Cielo restaurant ?

____

____

____

iii. What is 'Cave des Mousquetaires'?

____

____

____

Exercise 2

Match the following:

i.	Changi Airport	a.	TRECA® beds
ii.	Four Seasons Hotels and Resorts	b.	Singapore
iii.	Marais district	c.	Shops
iv.	Orchard MRT Station	d.	Canadian
v.	The Hotel de la Place du Louvre	e.	The Hilton Singapore

Discussion

You have been a trainee for a month at an international hotel. Talk to your group about the experience and work culture in a foreign land.

GRAMMAR BIN

Present Perfect Tense

The present perfect tense is used when:

a. The time period referred to has not finished. Example: *I **have seen** two films this week.* (This week has not finished yet.)

b. The time is not mentioned. Example: Kannan *has failed* his exam again.

c. The time is in the recent past. Example: She *has* just *completed* her graduation.

- *The present perfect is formed with have + past participle.*
- *Do not use used to and didn't together.*

We often come across people saying 'I didn't used to play music when I was a child'.

This is an incorrect usage.

The correct usage is 'I didn't play music when I was a child.'

Or, if it's a positive sentence, 'I used to play music when I was a child.'

Remember!

Exercise 1

Fill in the blanks with suitable forms of the verbs in the bracket:

i. Scientists ___________ (discover) the cure for this disease.

ii. We ___________ (solve) the main problem; there's nothing to worry about now.

iii. The price of real estate ___________ (increase) manifold within the last decade.

iv. I ___________ (complain) about this before, and will do so again.

v. My sister ___________ (be) to Brazil two times.

LANGUAGE FOCUS

Making Comparisons and Contrasts

Read the following passage on comparing and contrasting two fast food places:

> Let us first consider the size of the two places. Express King has 11,220 restaurants in 61 countries and The Big Chick has 30,000 in 119 countries. Both companies have been in business for 50 years although The Big Chick has had double of Express King's success.
>
> We would now compare menus, food and service quality of the two places. Although we prefer The Big Chick's food, the service is sometimes poor. But this is what you expect when they have such high revenues and high volume of customers each day. Express King's menu is not anything special, their food is good and their service is decent.
>
> The people who have seen Extra Large at The Big Chick know that there is nothing quite like it anywhere. Truly, today when one thinks of having a burger, The Big Chick is the first fast food restaurant that comes to mind.

Exercise 1

Make a presentation comparing and contrasting the service, food and ambience of any two major restaurants in your country.

Presenting the Right Image—Handling Complaints/Making Suggestions

Given here are some commonly used expressions on handling complaints and making suggestions:

i. **Please hold on:** Request which suggests that the caller wait for a while since the person at the other end of the line is busy.
ii. **Please:** Request for something.
iii. **I'm extremely sorry:** Apology.
iv. **I wonder if I could:** Starting to make a request.
v. **Goodbye:** Taking leave of someone.
vi. **Have a safe journey:** Wishing somebody who is going on a journey.
vii. **Would you kindly repeat that, sir/ma'am:** When you would like the guest to repeat what was said or when you do not understand what was said.
viii. **Certainly sir/ma'am, I will have housekeeping deliver it to your room:** When the guest asks for something that comes from another department.

Expressions of Politeness

We are aware that the hospitality industry values not only skilled professionals, but also those who are extremely courteous. Expressions of politeness, such as the following, always get appreciation for the speaker:

- Your complaint is justified and I shall look into the matter immediately.
- I'm extremely sorry, but the hotel is full. Would you please wait for a while?

Given below are some situations and the replies appropriate to them:

- **If you have to keep a guest waiting because you are busy with another guest**

Good morning, sir/ ma'am. I will be with you in a moment.

- **Then, when you revert to a guest**

I'm sorry to have kept you waiting, sir/ma'am. How may I assist you?

Exercise 1

Look at the following sentences and fill in the blanks with the appropriate phrases given in the box:

a. There seems to have been a mistake at our end.
b. We shall do our best to find it or get another one.
c. Kindly wait for a moment, we shall sort it out.
d. That's right. How can I help you?
e. Would you like something else instead?
f. May I call the doctor for you?

i. You are right about the missing statement, ____________
ii. Alpha Hotel? ____________
iii. We are so sorry about this confusion regarding your room, ____________
iv. It appears that there is an error in your bill, ____________
v. I am sorry to hear that. I hope you get well soon. ____________
vi. I am sorry, sir/ ma'am. This is not available____________

WORKPLACE SKILLS

Presentation

Can you think of popular songs which are played by your college/hotel band? Make a fun presentation with your partner about it. Try to engage the class in at least one activity during your presentation.

PRONUNCIATION

World Currencies

Practise the pronunciation of the following world currencies:

Dinar	Franc	Pound
Dirham	Krone	Ruble
Dollar	Lira	Taka
Euro	Peso	Yen

Case Studies

CASE STUDY 1

Catering to International Visitors

Look at the following list and tick all the directives that you follow or would want to follow in your profession:

- Meeting special requests of the guests.
- To serve an order to a guest in a restaurant, as ordered.
- Handling guest requests and complaints on priority and meeting his requirements.
- Immediately attending to any maintenance request.

What Would You Do?

A guest from an East European country has just arrived in your hotel. He speaks very little English and this is his first visit to your country. He does not have the currency of your country with him, and needs to exchange currency immediately.

Make groups of four and discuss this case. Then present your solutions before your class.

CASE STUDY 2

Meeting Guests' Expectations

It's good to exceed a guest's expectations because:

- It's free!
- It builds goodwill.
- It builds guest loyalty.
- It creates memorable experiences to be shared with others.
- It turns guests into ambassadors for the hotel.
- It leads to more business.
- It distinguishes our hotel from other hotels.

Remember the time when a guest mentioned you for exceptional service in his/her feedback? What did you do for them? How did it make you feel?

Make notes here:

Managing Elderly Guests

How will you provide extra care to elderly guests in your hotel? In the space given, write three precautions that you would take for them.

____

____

____

____

What Would You Do?

You have a 69-year-old guest in your hotel who is staying alone. One morning, when the maid knocks at his door there is no answer. The staff rings the room telephone and after several calls, decides to enter the room using the master key. They find the guest lying unconscious in the bathroom. What do you do now?

Make groups of four and discuss this case. Then present your solutions before your class.

CASE STUDY 3

Your Laundry, Please!

The staff in the housekeeping department know the importance of laundry in the hospitality business. Laundry requirements of guests change on a day-to-day basis and it is necessary to be attentive to their needs. Here are some of the aspects of laundry services an average hotel provides:

- Dry-cleaning
- Normal laundering
- Express laundry
- Ironing

What Would You Do?

It is important for housekeeping to make available to the guests fresh and clean linen.

Centralized laundries are a new trend in the industrial laundry business. While On Premise Laundries (OPLs) are energy and manpower intensive, centralized laundries allow hotel brands to save on capital and operation costs.

As the General Manager of your hotel you have to make a choice: your management favours the OPL system while the majority of the staff members insist on hiring the services of a centralized laundry. How would you make a decision? Make groups of four and discuss this case. Then present your solutions before your class.

CASE STUDY 4

Cheering for Teetotallers!

Teetotalism has received much encouragement after the expansion of coffee shops and juice bars across the country. Not only this, but of late we have been witnessing a proliferation of upmarket tea shops and mocktail outlets as well. Indeed, the fruit-based beverage industry is marching ahead thanks to a growing middle-class population and rapid urbanization.

Some popular non-alcoholic beverages are:

- Moroccan mint tea
- Chinese black keemun
- Blackberry juice
- Shakes/mocktails
- Lemonades
- Cold coffee
- Classic water

What Would You Do?

You have a group of high profile guests in your restaurant for dinner. Most of them order expensive wine, except one, who is a teetotaller. How would you serve this guest? Make groups of four and discuss this case. Then present your solutions before your class.

Appendix 1: Standard Polite Phrases

Communicating with guests is as much about building rapport as finding out or giving information.

You can build rapport by creating a sense of warmth and mutual respect. Greetings and pleasantries with guests can help build rapport, as can use of appropriate body language.

Greeting guests when you see them, using their name and exchanging pleasantries is part of good customer service. However, discretion is required to avoid over familiarity.

BASIC TIPS

These are some basic points which will help you improve your communication skills:

- While speaking to a guest, make sure that you maintain eye contact and smile. Maintain good posture, look alert and attentive.
- Always speak in complete sentences.
- Listen–do not just hear. Listen closely and be attentive to signs and tone of voice to understand what the guest wants.
- Be sure that the tone of your voice is pleasant and matches with what you wish to communicate.
- Use these magic words most often: 'please', 'thank you', 'excuse me', 'I'm sorry', 'I beg your pardon'.
- Use polite expressions such as 'may I', 'could I' and 'would you please' instead of 'can I/can you' and 'will you'.

Remember: Everything communicates!

POLITE PHRASES

Given here is a list of polite phrases which you can use in various situations.

SITUATION	RESPONSE
Greeting	Good morning, Sir/Ma'am. (00.00 hrs – 12.00 hrs) Good afternoon, Sir/Ma'am. (12.00 hrs – 16.00 hrs) Good evening, Sir/Ma'am. **Note:** It is wrong to say 'Morning, Sir/Madam'.
When you meet a repeat guest	Good morning Sir/Ma'am. It's good to see you again.
When leading a guest	Please come this way, Sir/Ma'am.
When an in-house guest is proceeding for his room from the restaurant, health club, business centre, etc.	Have a pleasant day, Sir/Madam. Have a pleasant afternoon, Sir/Madam. Good night, Sir/Madam. **Note:** Never say, 'Have a pleasant night.'

SITUATION	RESPONSE
Seeing a guest off	You can say any of the following: 1. Have a pleasant day, Sir/Ma'am. **OR** Have a pleasant afternoon, Sir/Ma'am. **OR** Good night, Sir/Ma'am. 2. We look forward to your next visit, Sir/Ma'am. 3. We are fortunate to serve you.
Asking the guest whether he needs any assistance	May I assist you, Sir/Madam?
Offering assistance	May I assist you, Sir/Ma'am? **OR** May I help you Sir/Ma'am/Mr ________? **OR** Allow me Sir/Ma'am (to carry his/her baggage, etc.)
When you want the guest to repeat what was said or when you do not understand what was said	I beg your pardon Sir/Ma'am. **OR** Would you kindly repeat that, Sir/Ma'am. **OR** Could you spell it for me, Sir/Ma'am?
When asking a guest his name	May I know your name please?
When a guest asks you the cost of something	That will be ₹ ________ inclusive/exclusive of tax.
When a guest asks for something	Certainly Sir/Ma'am, I will send it to your room.
When a guest asks for something that comes from another department	Certainly Sir/Ma'am. I will have Housekeeping deliver it to your room. **OR** Certainly Sir/Ma'am, our Systems manager will assist you. **OR** Certainly Sir/Ma'am, the Room Service attendant will come and help you.
When you are not able to provide the service requested by a guest	Mr/Ms ________ /Sir/Ma'am, please allow me to find out about it and I will get back to you. **OR** I am sorry, Sir/Ma'am/Mr/Ms ________. This is not available. May I get you ________ instead? **OR** I am sorry, Sir/Ma'am/Mr/Ms ________. This is not available. Would you like something else instead? **OR** I am terribly sorry, we do not have this item. Is there anything else we can provide?
When you are not sure whether something he has asked for can be provided	Mr/Ms ________ /Sir/Ma'am, please allow me to find out about it and get back to you.
When the guest is unwell	I am sorry to hear that. I hope you get well soon. May I call the doctor for you?
When a guest thanks you for something	We are fortunate to serve you, Sir/Ma'am.
If you have to inform Mr Sharma that his wife was looking for him.	Good morning Sir/Mr Sharma. Ma'am/Mrs Sharma had been looking for you.

SITUATION	RESPONSE
If you have to keep a guest waiting because you are busy with another guest.	Good morning Sir/Ma'am. I will be with you in a moment.
When you revert back to a guest	I'm sorry to have kept you waiting Sir/Ma'am. How may I assist you?

Remember: The key to communicating well lies in remembering the following questions:

WHAT? What do you really wish to communicate?
WHOM? To whom do you wish to communicate?
WHY? Why do you need to communicate?
HOW? How can you best communicate?
WHEN? When is the best time to communicate?

Appendix 2: Vocabulary Reference

IRREGULAR VERBS

INFINITIVE	PAST FORM	PAST PARTICIPLE	INFINITIVE	PAST FORM	PAST PARTICIPLE
arise	Arose	Arisen	dig	Dug	Dug
awake	Awoke	Awoken	dive	Dived, (AM) dove	dived
be	Was, were	Been	do	Did	Done
beat	Beat	Beaten	draw	Drew	Drawn
become	Became	Become	dream	Dreamed or dreamt	Dreamed or dreamt
begin	Began	Begun	drink	Drank	drunk
bend	Bent	Bent	drive	Drove	driven
bet	Bet	Bet	Eat	Ate	Eaten
bind	Bound	Bound	Fall	Fell	Fallen
bite	Bit	Bitten	Feed	Fed	Fed
bleed	Bled	Bled	Feel	Felt	Felt
blow	Blew	Blown	Fight	Fought	Fought
break	Broke	Broken	Find	Found	Found
bring	Brought	Brought	Fly	Flew	Flown
build	Built	Built	Forbid	Forbade	forbidden
burn	Burned or burnt	Burned or burnt	Forget	Forgot	Forgotten
burst	Burst	Burst	Freeze	Froze	Frozen
buy	Bought	Bought	Get	Got	Got (AM) gotten
can	Could	–	Give	Gave	Given
cast	Cast	Cast	Go	Went	Gone
catch	Caught	Caught	Grind	Ground	Ground
choose	Chose	Chosen	Grow	Grew	Grown
cling	Clung	Clung	Hang	Hung or hanged	Hung or hanged
come	Came	Come	Have	Had	Had
cost	Cost or costed	Cost or costed	Hear	Heard	Heard
creep	Crept	Crept	Hide	Hid	Hidden
cut	Cut	Cut	Hit	Hit	Hit
deal	Dealt	Dealt	Hold	Held	Held

INFINITIVE	PAST FORM	PAST PARTICIPLE	INFINITIVE	PAST FORM	PAST PARTICIPLE
Hurt	Hurt	Hurt	Shed	Shed	Shed
Keep	Kept	Kept	Shine	Shone or shined	Shone or shined
Kneel	Knelt or kneeled	Knelt or kneeled	Shoe	Shod	Shod
Know	Knew	Known	Shoot	Shot	Shot
Lay	Laid	Laid	Show	Showed	Shown
Lead	Led	Led	Shrink	Shrank	Shrunk
Lean	Leaned or leant	Leaned or leant	Shut	Shut	Shut
Leap	Leaped or leapt	Leaped or leapt	Sing	Sang	Sung
Learn	Learned or learnt	Learned or learnt	Sink	Sank	Sunk
Leave	Left	Left	Sit	Sat	Sat
Lend	Lent	Lent	Sleep	Slept	Slept
Let	Let	let	Slide	Slid	Slid
lie	Lay	Lain	Smell	Smelled or smelt	Smelled or smelt
Light	Lit or lighted	Lit or lighted	Speak	Spoke	Spoken
Lose	Lost	Lost	Speed	Speeded or sped	Speeded or sped
Make	Made	Made	Spell	Spelled or spelt	Spelled or spelt
May	Might	–	Spend	Spent	Spent
Mean	Meant	Meant	Spill	Spilled or spilt	Spilled or spilt
Meet	Met	Met	Spit	Spat, (American: spit)	(AM) spit
Pay	Paid	Paid	Spoil	Spoiled or spoilt	Spoiled or spoilt
Put	Put	Put	Spread	Spread	Spread
Quit	Quit	Quit	Spring	Sprang	Sprung
Read	read	read	Stand	Stood	Stood
Rid	Rid	Rid	Steal	Stole	stolen
Ride	Rode	Ridden	Stick	Stuck	Stuck
ring	Rang	rung	Sting	Stung	Stung
Rise	Rose	Risen	Stink	Stank	Stunk
Run	Ran	Run	Strike	Struck	Struck or stricken
Say	Said	Said	Swear	Swore	Sworn
See	Saw	Seen	Sweep	Swept	Swept
Seek	Sought	Sought	Swell	Swelled	Swollen
Sell	Sold	Sold	Swim	Swam	Swum
Send	Sent	Sent	Swing	Swung	Swung
set	Set	Set	Take	Took	taken
Shake	Shook	Shaken	Teach	Taught	Taught

INFINITIVE	PAST FORM	PAST PARTICIPLE	INFINITIVE	PAST FORM	PAST PARTICIPLE
tear	Tore	Torn	Wear	Wore	Worn
Tell	Told	Told	Weep	Wept	Wept
Think	Thought	Thought	Win	Won	Won
Throw	Threw	Thrown	Wind	Wound	Wound
Wake	Woke, (AM) waked	Woken	write	Wrote	written

BRITISH AND AMERICAN SPELLINGS

ENGLISH	AMERICAN ENGLISH	ENGLISH	AMERICAN ENGLISH
acknowledgement	acknowledgment	licence (verb and noun)	license (verb and noun)
analyse	analyze	litre	liter
centre	center	metre	meter
cheque	check	mould	mold
colour	color	neighbour	neighbor
counsellor	counselor	offence	offense
criticise, criticize	criticize	practise (verb)	practice (verb)
defence	defense	pretence	pretense
doughnut	donut	programme	program
favour	favor	pyjamas	pajamas
fibre	fiber	realise, realize	realize
flavour	flavor	savour	savor
fulfil	fulfill	speciality	specialty
grey	gray	theatre	theater
honour	honor	travelled	traveled
humour	humor	travelling	traveling
jewellery	jewelry	tyre	tire
labour	labor	valour	valor

Units of Measurement

Volume

10 millilitres (ml) = 1 centilitre (cl)
10 centilitres = 1 decilitre (dl) = 100 millilitres
10 decilitres = 1 litre = 1000 millilitres

10 litres	= 1 dekaliter (dal)
10 dekalitres	= 1 hectoliter (hl) = 100 litres
10 hectolitres	= 1 kiloliter (kl) = 1000 litres

Mass

10 milligrams (mg)	= 1 centigram (cg)
10 centigrams	= 1 decigram (dg) = 100 milligrams
10 decigrams	= 1 gram (g) = 1000 milligrams
10 grams	= 1 dekagram (dag)
10 dekagrams	= 1 hectogram (hg) = 100 grams
10 hectograms	= 1 kilogram (kg) = 1000 grams
1000 kilograms	= 1 megagram (Mg) or 1 metric tonne

Length

12 inches (in)	= 1 foot (ft)
3 feet	= 1 yard (yd)
16.5 feet	= 1 rod (rd), polé, or perch
40 rods	= 1 furlong (fur) = 660 feet
8 furlongs	= 1 US statute mile (mi) = 5280 feet
1852 meters	= 6076.115 49 feet (approximately)
	= 1 international nautical mile

Listening Exercises

Listen to the passages in the CD provided along with the book and complete the activities given below.

ACTIVITY 1

1. Listen to Passage 1 on the CD and answer the following questions:
   i. What's the name of the hotel?
   ii. Who are the two people talking?
   iii. When will the speaker arrive at the hotel?
   iv. What is the most special quality of the hotel?
2. State whether the following are true or false:
   i. The two museums mentioned are Louvre and Galerie Pierre–Alain.
   ii. Bosco Bazar is ideal for shopping for children's wear.
   iii. Hotel Villa Rose is known for its vast library.

ACTIVITY 2

1. Listen to Passage 2 on the CD and answer the following questions:
   i. What are the highlights of the Sapphire Suite?
   ii. Which are the television channels available in the hotel?
   iii. Which are the news channels that the hotel TV shows?
   iv. Which are the blocked channels in this hotel?
2. Fill in the blanks:
   i. The Sapphire Suite offers Italian crockery, and _________ bath linen.
   ii. The hotel provides an iHome _________ next to the guest's bed.
   iii. The hotel is the right choice for those addicted to _________.

ACTIVITY 3

1. Listen to Passage 3 on the CD and answer the following questions:
   i. Who is a successful entrepreneur?
   ii. Why is Donald Trump so successful?
   iii. What is the secret of Bill Marriott's success?
   iv. What is the place of Mohan Singh Oberoi in the hotel industry of India?

2. State whether the following are true or false:

   i. India's first 5 star hotel was launched in the year 1963.

   ii. Oberoi School of Hotel Management is recognized by the International Hotel Association in Paris.

   iii. Donald Trump appears in a popular TV show called *The Entourage*

ACTIVITY 4

1. Listen to Passage 4 on the CD and answer the following questions:

   i. Why is Warsaw important as a tourist spot?

   ii. What is the Palace of Culture and Science?

   iii. What is the famous cuisine of Poland?

   iv. Who was Frédéric Chopin?

   v. What are the features of the Bristol Hotel?

2. Fill in the blanks:

   i. Warsaw was destroyed during the _________ reign.

   ii. Bristol Hotel has _________ Star ratings.

   iii. Poland is known for its _________ bars.

ACTIVITY 5

1. Listen to Passage 5 on the CD and answer the following questions:

   i. Where is the Heathrow Airport?

   ii. Name some of the hotels around the Heathrow Hotel.

   iii. How far is the Premier Inn located from the Heathrow airport?

   iv. Which is the cheapest hotel near the airport?

   v. What is the customer rating for the Renaissance Hotel?

2. Fill in the blanks:

   i. Yotel was founded by _________ and Gerard Greene.

   ii. The Renaissance London Heathrow, a 4-star hotel situated on the _________.

   iii. On a scale of 1 to 5, The Renaissance is given _________.

ACTIVITY 6

1. Listen to Passage 6 on the CD and answer the following questions:

   i. What are the features of the Crown Plaza Changi Airport?

   ii. How does one reach the main city from the airport?

   iii. What are the highlights of the Transit Hotel at the airport?

2. Fill in the blanks:

    i. Crowne Plaza Changi Airport's stunning exterior consists of a ________ of tropical flowers.
    ii. At the Crowne Plaza, guests can pick their own fish from the tank and dine ________ at Imperial Treasure.
    iii. Four Seasons Hotel Singapore is situated along the tree-lined ________.

ACTIVITY 7

1. Listen to Passage 7 on the CD and answer the following questions:

    i. What are the common features of a green hotel?
    ii. What is the role of the bamboo grove in helping the environment?
    iii. Whar are eco tent cottages?

2. State whether the following are true or false:

    i. The Gyreum Ecolodge is the first lodge in Asia to be awarded the EU Eco Label.
    ii. ITC Maurya is acclaimed for its in-hotel restaurants Bukhara and Sagar Ratna.
    iii. Hotel Rafayel promotes bus tours to explore London.

ACTIVITY 8

1. Listen to Passage 8 on the CD and answer the following questions:

    i. How strong is the inn culture in Britain?
    ii. What are the features of the Swan Inn?
    iii. Mention any two highlights of the Bishop's Castle.

2. Fill in the blanks:

    i. Keswick is also known as the ________.
    ii. LakeSide House is in the vicinity of the bustling ________.
    iii. Bishop's Castle is located halfway between ________.

ACTIVITY 9

1. Listen to Passage 9 on the CD and answer the following questions:

    i. List the ingredients of Golden Opulence Sundae.
    ii. What is the specialty of Frozen Haute Chocolate?
    iii. Why is the steak and mushroom pie so expensive?

2. State whether the following are true or false:

    i. For the mushroom pie, the chef used Chateau Mouton Rothschild wine.
    ii. Frozen Haute Chocolate is created in partnership with luxury jeweler Euphoria.
    iii. The Japanese Matsutake mushroom can be easily cultivated anywhere in the world.

Audio Scripts

LISTENING EXERCISE 1

Hi. My name is Sophie Ali and I am an interior designer. Today I am leaving for Paris, which is one of my favourite destinations across the globe. I think Paris offers the best shopping experience than anywhere else. Consider the flea market on the Rue des Rosiers, which caters to both alternative and traditional tastes and offers a range of vintage markets, boutiques and galleries. I feel there is something different and original to be discovered each time I am there. In Paris I will be staying at Villa Rose, which is luxurious and has a wonderful ambience. I am taking the Virgin Atlantic from London to Paris and will arrive at Paris at 19.00 hours this Thursday. In Paris, I am looking forward to visiting the Louvre and Galerie Pierre–Alain and shopping at Champs Elyseé. Champs Elyseé is a famous street and you will find it featured in several French films. If you are looking for some great stores, then I would suggest Merci, a store that has it all. Bonton Bazar, on the other hand is for children's wear, and Le Bon Marché is simply the best department store one could wish for.

While in Paris, I never miss a walk on the pavements and sitting for hours together in the celebrated cafes. Just a block from the Louvre, is Café Plat which stocks more than 20 varieties of single-origin beans and house blends, freshly roasted with an intoxicating aroma. It also operates as a quaint salon de café, where you can sample the coffee of your choice with an optional slice of cake. The café provides a wonderful view of the Arch de Triomphe.

Villa Rose is also known for its vast library. In fact each of its 35 rooms is devoted to a letter of the alphabet. Homer and Rousseau are honoured in the H and R rooms, with quotes from their famous works adorning the walls. Velvet and wood décor gives the rooms an old world charm. Set in the 6th arrondisement, Villa Rose is a great hangout for booklovers in Paris.

LISTENING EXERCISE 2

Welcome to Hotel Royal Taj, a 15 acre spread of pure luxury. Only a 20 minutes drive from the international airport, we provide an ideal lodging for business travellers who check in for its quiet charm. And we offer pick up and drop facility in a swanky Mercedes to treat you like royalty. Now let me tell you about some of our highlights. The Sapphire Suite is perched high above the city and will appeal to all those who appreciate good taste. The living room's floor-to-ceiling windows look out on to the lush garden and the pool. The suite is grand yet offers the comfort of your home. It offers Italian crockery, Frette bath linen, a kitchenette, 24 hours butler service and a walk-in closet.

For your entertainment, our suites are equipped with a parlour-type living room with a couch, chair, 36 inch flatscreen TV, and a DVD player with an assortment of DVDs. We offer you an astounding range of national and international television channels. This includes HBO, Star World, CNN-IBN, BBC, and all the major sports and news channels, in addition to an iHome iPod dock next to your bed. Some channels airing adult contents are blocked, however.

If you are a spa addict, you have chosen the right hotel. We have been voted as among the top 15 best spas in the world, and include an array of treatments. The spa experts have won several major awards for their skills and you will certainly be safe in their hands.

For the gourmand in you, we invite you to savour the best of Indian cuisine. While our Mughlai chef would settle for nothing less than royal recipes, our chef Lee is known for his signature Oriental dishes. If you want to enjoy a full Italian meal, head to Caraviggio to take in the city skyline and dine on fine Italian cuisine.

LISTENING EXERCISE 3

Great businesses are as much a matter of luck and hard work as about the right timing. The adventurous streak and the ability to take risks—calculated or otherwise—work big time if only there is a vision to support these. Think , for instance, how Mohan Singh Oberoi became the first Indian hotelier to enter into an agreement with an internationally renowned hotel chain, and launched the first modern, five-star hotel in the country in 1965. The Oberoi Inter-continental, or the I-Con, as it became famous as it offered unprecedented facilities and soon became India's premier luxury hotel. This achievement was crowned with the opening of the 35-storey Oberoi Sheraton in Mumbai, in 1973. Oberoi was the first Indian to work in association with international chains to attract international travellers to India. Another 'first' was the establishment of the prestigious Oberoi School of Hotel Management, recognized by the International Hotel Association in Paris.

Brothers Bill and Richard belong to the illustrious Marriott family, where Bill Marriott, Jr. is Executive Chairman and Chairman of the Board of Marriott International, Inc., one of the world's largest hospitality companies. Under his leadership Marriott went from a family restaurant business to become a global lodging company with more than 3,700 branches in all major countries. Appreciated for his hands-on management style, Bill Marriott has built one of the most well regarded hotel cultures across the globe.

America's leading business entrepreneur, author, socialite and television personality Donald Trump owes his success to dreaming big and building a larger than life persona. He is the Chairman and CEO of the Trump Organization, as well as a famous real-estate developer. Donald is also the founder of Trump Entertainment Resorts, a company that operates a multiplicity of casinos and hotels all around the world. Trump's enviable lifestyle and charismatic personality has made him a celebrity, and his phenomenally popular reality television show, *The Apprentice,* has cemented this status. 'Think big, take risks and never be afraid of failing,' is what Trump lives by.

LISTENING EXERCISE 4

Warsaw is the beautiful capital of Poland. Currently in the process of repairing and reconstructing itself in the aftermath of Communist Soviet supremacy, Warsaw is fast becoming the economic centre of Poland, along with gaining recognition as a historically important city. As part of the capital's effort to regain its cultural glory, the city celebrated the great musician Frédéric Chopin's 200th birth anniversary. Warsaw created a special walking route through the city, where audio guides were provided on the route and a host of musicians played some of Chopin's most famous pieces , while also giving information about the spot and its connection to the classical composer. We also recommend a visit to the Palace of Culture and Science, Poland's tallest building at 756 feet, which offers great views from the 30th floor. The area near the monument is a haven for avid shoppers.

While not exactly known for its cuisine, Poland , however, is famous for its milk bars. These small eateries serve traditional items such as Pierogies: baked or fried dumplings; stuffed with potato, meat, cheese or fruit.

Bristol Hotel is situated on Warsaw's fashionable "Royal Route," the road that leads through the historical area of the city. The Hotel gives a view of the Presidential Palace and has some of the capital city's finest architecture, including magnificent palaces, churches, and statues in its vicinity. The hotel's features and amenities include meeting and banquet facilities for events of all scales and the Cafe Bristol featuring the finest in Viennese-style cuisine. With 5 star ratings, Bristol is the last word in luxury hotels in Warsaw.

LISTENING EXERCISE 5

Welcome to the Heathrow Airport, one of the best-known airports in the world. Heathrow has a number of hotels in its vicinity, both luxury and budget. The Premier Inn is one such reasonably priced place where you can spend a night before taking a flight. Conveniently situated on Bath Road, just one mile away from the airport, the Premier Inn Heathrow Airport Hotel, makes it possible to opt for park and fly packages that arrange for your car to be securely parked near our hotel for the duration of your trip away. Additionally, our Heathrow Airport Hotel provides for endless wireless internet access and connectivity. At Bath Road, we offer a modern business lounge and hot desks. Moreover, our close proximity with the Heathrow Express rail connection ensures that business and leisure travellers staying at our hotels will find getting to the airport in time for their flight easy.

The Crown Plaza Hotel London Heathrow is located only 20 minutes drive away from central London. All rooms consist of cable TV, in-room movies, a large work desk, excellent internet access, minibar, coffee/tea maker and a bathroom, fitted with all amenities. With £30 per night, it is also the cheapest hotel available in that area.

And now let's talk about Yotel. As you would know, Yotel is a YO! Company hotel brand with hotels at airports, founded by Simon Woodruff and Gerard Greene. The Heathrow Airport hotel is located inside Terminal 4 to give travellers the ultimate experience of being only minutes away from departures and arrival gates. This is an extraordinary hotel experience at a great value. The very comfortable 'cabins' can be booked by the hour with check-in and check-out times totally flexible according to your convenience. We also provide free wi-fi and hot drinks. 'Food to Go' is available round the clock, which you can order from our menu at the Galley. So the next time you have an early flight, a stopover or are in transit, you know where to go for a few hours to relax, refresh, connect and sleep before your onward journey.

And lastly, we will move on to the Renaissance London Heathrow, a 4-star hotel situated on the A4. The hotel gives you a breathtaking view of the main runway, modern interiors, excellent service, and comfortable, soundproof guest rooms. The hotel is a perfect base for a pleasant stay. The health club offers a selection of relaxing treatments and a 24/7 fitness centre.

The Renaissance London Heathrow Hotel offers several places to dine. For events of medium and large magnitude, the hotel offers meeting and conference facilities, including the tiered York Auditorium. No wonder, on a scale of 1 to 5, our customers have given us 4.5 points!

LISTENING EXERCISE 6

Getting to and from Changi Airport is easy with regular and affordable public transport. A convenient range of parking options is available, which includes airport shuttles, buses, car rental, coach, ground transport desk, taxis and trains.

The Crowne Plaza Changi Airport is located within the immediate vicinity of Changi Airport. Linked to Terminal 3, the nine-storey hotel has 320 guest rooms; a spacious Crowne Plaza Club Lounge and executive class amenities such as restaurants, meeting rooms, conference rooms, spa lounges, a swimming pool and a health and fitness club. The ultra-modern Airport hotel is 25 minutes' drive from the city.

Crowne Plaza Airport's stunning exterior consists of a metallic latticework of tropical flowers, a motif that is present in the hotel's sharply modern interior. Your eye will be drawn to the curvaceous sofas, inspired by papaya and watermelon, in our futuristic lobby. To quickly freshen up, head straight to your room for a relaxing shower or retreat to our sumptuous spa for a range of massage treatments.

A link bridge connects Crowne Plaza Changi Airport to Changi Airport's Terminal 3. We are just 10 minutes from Changi Business Park, home to banks and multinationals, and you can reach the city by taxi in 25 minutes. Once inside, discover our tropical resort, with courtyard gardens and a landscaped pool area. You'll find peaceful garden views from the Lobby Lounge or in our al fresco courtyard. And what's more, we invite you to pick your own fish from the tank and dine Cantonese-style at Imperial Treasure.

Changi Airport is very conscious of its commitment towards its customers. The Transit Hotel at the airport is equipped with a television, en suite bathroom and more, we make sure you have everything you need for a comfortable stay. There's also a wake-up call service at your requested time, so you don't have to worry about missing your flight.

Another landmark hotel in Singapore is the Four Seasons Hotel. The 20-storey building along the tree-lined Orchard Boulevard is a luxury five-star hotel just minutes from shopping centres, family attractions and the city's bustling financial district. A world-class hotel, Four Seasons is the preferred choice of the crème de la crème of the international community.

LISTENING EXERCISE 7

Welcome to the world of green hotels. You might be aware that a hotel which practises conservation of water, fuel and energy is popularly known as a green hotel. Green hotels are also committed to installing systems that help reduce, reuse and recycle waste.

One of the most eco-friendly lodgings in the world, the Gyreum Ecolodge is the first lodge in Europe to be awarded the EU Eco Label and was shortlisted for the LAMA Award as the Best Ecofriendly Building. This solar and wind powered circular fort is located in County Sligo and constructed from renewable resources. Rafayel on the Left Bank in Battersea, London is a luxury eco hotel that does not compromise on quality and comfort when going green. Guests can enjoy a bamboo grove that has been planted to release a higher quantity of oxygen than many other tree types, as well as organic spa treatments, fair-trade mini-bar treats, and wines and cocktails that have been produced using farm-to-bar methods. A major feature is that Rafayel promotes cycling tours to explore London.

The ITC Maurya, New Delhi is a swanky hotel that is popular with executives and dignitaries. The self-proclaimed 'Greenest Luxury Hotel in the World' was given the US Green Building Council's Leadership in Energy and Environmental Design (LEED EB) award in 2010. Some of the major initiatives include a 'Reduce, Reuse, Recycle' programme, getting suppliers to adopt cleaner and environmental friendly methods , and creating water and energy games that are both educational and entertaining.

The ITC Maurya is acclaimed for its in-hotel restaurants Bukhara and Dum Pukht. Guests can be assured that their food is fresh and healthy, as about 40 per cent of ingredients used are harvested locally and cooked using solar power.

Likewise, The Imperial, Delhi too has recently inaugurated the solar panels for heating water in guest rooms. What's more, the suppliers have been instructed to reduce packaging material and recycle paper. The hotel is also soon to introduce biogas plants for effective waste management. It is also one of the premier hotels to observe Earth Hour every week where lights are switched off in many areas of the property for one hour.

Eco tent cottages is a revolutionary concept for the hotel industry. The concept is ideal for beach resorts, safari tents, holiday villas, retreat cabins, prefab structures, and customized buildings. These structures are furnished with a range of eco-amenities such as solar power and natural ventilation, along with all the facilities of a concrete structure making it a perfect package to meet the demands of urban lifestyle.

LISTENING EXERCISE 8

Britain is known for its great inn culture. Britain's finest small hotels and inns include over 400 traditional hotels and inns, country house hotels, town house hotels, boutique hotels and restaurants with rooms, ranging from modest accommodation to establishments of immense luxury. There is strong geographical coverage across the United Kingdom, so whether you are searching for small hotels in York, comfortable Welsh hotels, Lancashire hotels or cosy places in Essex, you will find the right place to suit your taste and budget.

The Swan Inn is set in the Surrey countryside , bordering West Sussex, an ideal retreat with unfussy service and great attention to detail. The spacious and individually furnished bedrooms are luxurious and offer every home comfort. Savour the delicious food on offer in the restaurant, the talented chef creates simple, yet delicious menus around the very best local produce. The private dining room is perfect for a special celebration or corporate event, tailor-made to suit your taste and occasion.

LakeSide House has been renovated to offer luxurious contemporary boutique accommodation for visitors seeking a special stay in The Lakes. The restoration has been meticulously detailed and sympathetic to the buildings classical Victorian heritage. The high quality rooms are individually designed and each have a contemporary en-suite flat screen digital TV, tea and coffee making facilities, ample wardrobe storage and pocket sprung beds. Situated on the south edge of Keswick, LakeSide House is in the vicinity of the bustling town centre. The place offers bicycle storage, a cloak and drying room, and is ideally located for the endless activities Keswick, better known as Britain's adventure capital, has to offer. Breakfast is served in a bright open dining room with large bay windows that open to the breathtaking backdrop of stunning scenery of the North Lakes. All of our produce is sourced locally where possible and is freshly prepared by the chef each morning.

The Castle Hotel is located in a quiet square in the small market town of Bishop's Castle, halfway between Shrewsbury and Ludlow. In the heart of the Shropshire Hills there is much to explore, both in Shropshire and neighbouring Wales. It is surrounded by great walking country. The eight en-suite bedrooms are individually furnished, some with the breathtaking views of the town, and the countryside. There is a choice of eating venues, each with its own character and all serving food that is wholesome and fresh. The hotel gardens provide a great vantage point to view the surrounding hills, preferably with a glass of something inebriating in hand and the promise of dinner in the air. Bishops Castle is a delightful little town, with a strong arts and crafts tradition and plenty of antique shops and tea rooms to explore.

LISTENING EXERCISE 9

Whoever said that fine dining is affordable needs to think twice! After all, how much can a goblet of sundae cost? Well, Serendipity 3 of Upper East Side, New York created the most extravagant ice-cream sundae to celebrate their 50th anniversary. The sundae consists of five scoops of Tahitian vanilla bean ice-cream infused with vanilla from Madagascar, peppered with Amedei Porcelana chocolate, tiny bits of Chuao chocolate from Venezuela and 23 carat edible gold leaf. Add a dash of candied fruit from Paris, truffles and cherries, and top it all with a bowl of Grand Passion caviar , this sundae , quite appropriately named Golden Opulence Sundae is priced at $1000. However, this was not the epitome of culinary indulgence. Serendipity is also credited with creating a $25,000 Frozen Haute Chocolate in partnership with luxury jeweller Euphoria. The dessert is made from almost 30 kinds of cocoa, many of which are the most expensive. To infuse that extra something, it has a gold bracelets with diamonds placed at the bottom.

Founded by Calvin Holt in 1954, the eatery was named Serendipity because of its romantic meaning: the art of finding the pleasantly unexpected by chance or sagacity. Coined by eighteenth century scholar Sir Horace Walpole, it evoked the ancient legend of the three princes of the island once known as Serendip.

Would you believe it if I tell you that a mushroom pie can cost you $15,900? This is how it works: the Japanese Matsutake mushroom is extremely hard to harvest and can come to $2000 per kg. In the year 2005, Chef Spence Burge of the Fence Gate Inn in Lancashire used these mushrooms to give us the world's most expensive steak and mushroom pie. The recipe involved British classics such as Wagyu beef and black truffles. The sauce was made from 1982 Chateau Mouton Rothschild wine and was topped with gold leaf. And the price of this sumptuous decadence? Just $15,900. So let's say bon appetit and bon vivre to that!

Credits

Every effort has been made to obtain permission from all copyright holders, but in some cases this has not proved possible. The publishers therefore wish to thank all authors and copyright holders who are included without acknowledgement. Dorling Kindersley India (Pvt.) Ltd., licencees of Pearson Education in India, apologize for any errors and omissions in this list and would be grateful to be notified of any corrections that should be incorporated in the next edition.

TEXT CREDITS

Chapter 1

Page 12: 'London', by William Blake, taken from *Songs of Experience*, published in 1794.

Chapter 2

Page 16: 'Handshake or Hug? Knowing Intercultural Greetings', adapted from an article accessed at http://www.bpic.co.uk/articles/greetings.html on 30 January 2013.
Page 22: 'Westminster Bridge', by William Wordsworth, taken from *The Complete Poetical Works* (London: Macmillan and Co., 1888).

Chapter 3

Page 28: 'Hotel and Tourism: A Booming Industry', adapted from an article accessed at http://www.iloveindia.com on 20 January 2013.

Chapter 4

Page 41: 'Elevator Etiquette', adapted from an article accessed at http://www.wisegeek.com on 20 January 2013.

Chapter 5

Page 54: 'Room Service Takes A New Turn', adapted from an article accessed at www.executivetravel-magazine.com on 20 January 2013.
Page 61: 'Entrepreneurship: How Do They Get There?' taken from Upendra Kachru, *India: Land of A Billion Entrepreneurs* (New Delhi: Dorling Kindersley (India) Pvt. Ltd., 2011).

Chapter 6

Page 71: 'When Things Go Way Wrong In Our Workplace', taken from Gopalaswamy Ramesh and Mahadevan Ramesh, *The Ace of Soft Skills: Attitude, Communication and Etiquette for Success* (New Delhi: Dorling Kindersley (India) Pvt. Ltd., 2011).

Chapter 9

Page 104: 'Hotel Lobbies As Social Spaces', adapted from an article accessed at http://www.readwriteweb.com/enterprise/2011/09/hotel-lobbies-become-more-soci.php on 20 January 2013.
Page 107: 'Are you ready for soft skills?', taken from Gopalaswamy Ramesh and Mahadevan Ramesh, *The Ace of Soft Skills: Attitude, Communication and Etiquette for Success* (New Delhi: Dorling Kindersley (India) Pvt. Ltd., 2011).
Page 111: 'The Phantom Luncheon', taken from Saki, *The Toys of Peace, and other papers* (London: John Lane, 1919).

Chapter 10

Page 119: 'The Vigeland Park', adapted from an article accessed at http://www.vigeland.museum.no/en/vigeland-park/ 20 January 2013.

Chapter 12

Page 145: 'A Room With A View', excerpted from E. M. Forster, *A Room With A View* (Norfolk: Alfred A. Knopf Inc., 1922).

Chapter 13

Page 151: 'Cars for Hire', adapted from the article 'Welcome to Cars Rental India' accessed at http://www.carsrentalindia.net/ on 25 January 2013.

Chapter 14

Page 165: 'Dusk', taken from Saki, *Beasts and Superbeasts* (London: John Lane The Bodley Head, 1914).

IMAGE CREDITS

Chapter 1

Page 5: Hotel bedroom, from Shutterstock.

Chapter 2

Page 14: Guests being welcomed at front desk, from Shutterstock.

Chapter 3

Page 23: Handing over keys, from Shutterstock.

Chapter 4

Page 38: In the lift, from Shutterstock.

Chapter 5

Page 56: Bathrooms, courtesy of Geetika Malik.

Chapter 6

Page 65: Food platter, from Shutterstock.

Chapter 7

Page 77: Conference table in front of the ocean, from Shutterstock.

Chapter 8

Page 90: Gateway to India at Sunset in Mumbai, from Shutterstock.
Page 95: Person writing from Shutterstock.

Chapter 9

Page 101: Hotel reception, courtesy Deepti Goel.
Page 104: Hotel lobby, from Shutterstock.

Chapter 10

Page 115: People arguing, courtesy Insiya Poonawala.

Chapter 11

Page 124: Restaurant table, from Shutterstock.

Chapter 13

Page 155: Taxi, from Shutterstock.

Chapter 14

Page 165: Taking a message at the reception, from Shutterstock.
Page 171: Hotel room, from Shutterstock.

Chapter 15

Page 177: Checking out of a hotel room, from Shutterstock.

